Hume's Moral Theory

International Library of Philosophy

Editor: Ted Honderich

A catalogue of books already published in the
International Library of Philosophy
will be found at the end of this volume

Hume's Moral Theory

J. L. Mackie

ROUTLEDGE & KEGAN PAUL

London, Boston and Henley

First published in 1980
by Routledge & Kegan Paul Ltd
39 Store Street, London WC1E 7DD,
9 Park Street, Boston, Mass. 02108, USA and
Broadway House, Newtown Road, Henley-on-Thames, Oxon RG9 1EN
Set in Times 10 on 12 pt by
Computacomp (UK) Ltd,
Fort William, Scotland
and printed in Great Britain by
Page Bros. (Norwich) Ltd
Norwich, Norfolk

British Library Cataloguing in Publication Data

Mackie, John Leslie

Hume's moral theory. – (International library of
philosophy).
1. Hume, David – Ethics
2. Ethics
I. Title II. Series
170'.92'4   B1499.E8   79–41565

ISBN 0 7100 0524 5
ISBN 0 7100 0525 3 Pbk

CONTENTS

Preface vii

I Introduction: Outline of Hume's Theory 1

II Some Predecessors: Hobbes, Shaftesbury, Clarke, Wollaston, Mandeville, Hutcheson, Butler 7

III Hume's Psychology of Action (*Treatise* II iii 3) 44

IV Morality not Based on Reason (*Treatise* III i 1) 51

V Variants of Sentimentalism (*Treatise* III i 2) 64

VI The Artificial Virtues 76
 1 Justice and Property (*Treatise* III ii 1–4) 76
 2 The Obligation of Promises (*Treatise* III ii 5) 96
 3 The Artificiality of Justice (*Treatise* III ii 6) 104
 4 The Origin of Government and the Limits of Political Obligation (*Treatise* III ii 7–10) 106
 5 International Justice (*Treatise* III ii 11) 113
 6 Chastity and Modesty (*Treatise* III ii 12) 118

VII The Natural Virtues (*Treatise* III iii 1–5) 120

VIII Some Successors: Smith, Price, Reid 130

IX Conclusions 145

Notes 157

Index 163

PREFACE

Hume's moral theory has been relatively neglected, as compared with some other parts of his philosophy. Indeed, all that many reasonably well-informed students of philosophy know about it is that he said (or, alternatively, that he did not say) that you cannot derive an 'ought' from an 'is'. But Hume's Law, as this has been called, is not the whole, or even the most important part, of his moral theory. It is compatible with an objectivist or intuitionist view which Hume would certainly have rejected, and it contains no hint of his fascinating account of what he called the artificial virtues, or of his anticipations of utilitarianism, to which Bentham ascribed his own conversion to that doctrine. Also, Hume's theory is best seen in the context of, and as a contribution to, an extended debate on moral philosophy which we can take as beginning with Hobbes, being continued by members of both the 'rationalist' and the 'moral sense' or 'sentimentalist' schools, and concluding with the writings of two of Hume's critics, Richard Price and Thomas Reid. Some of the main issues in this debate are whether there are, or are not, objective moral values, whether men are by nature completely selfish or are 'made for society', whether morality depends in any way upon God and religion, and how and by what faculty we discern the difference between vice and virtue. The works in which this debate was carried on were addressed to an educated general public rather than to specialists in philosophy, and they are written in a straightforward, forthright way, without technicalities or obfuscation or evasion. They are not free from errors and fallacies, but where they go wrong they do so openly, and their mistakes are often pointed out by other participants in the debate. I think, therefore, that attention to this debate is a very good method of learning at least part of the core of moral philosophy – for example, learning to distinguish moral phenomenology, the description of our ordinary moral experience and concepts and beliefs, from questions about the status of moral judgments and the explanation at a deeper level of moral thinking as a whole. Moreover, adequate selections from the works of these writers are readily available in D. D. Raphael's *British Moralists 1650–1800* (Oxford, 1969), where most of the passages I quote or refer to can be found. I hope that my book will encourage readers to go further into the writings not only of Hume himself, but also of his predecessors and successors.

An important exception to the general neglect of Hume's moral theory is the thorough examination of one part of it by Jonathan Harrison in *Hume's Moral Epistemology* (Oxford, 1976). My own discussion owes a good deal to this, and also to another, not yet published, work in which Harrison examines with the same thoroughness the other main parts of Hume's theory. But there are, naturally enough, some points on which I disagree with Harrison. An earlier book which deals very clearly with one theme in the debate among the British moralists, and relates it to what G. E. Moore called 'the naturalistic fallacy', is Arthur Prior's *Logic and the Basis of Ethics* (Oxford, 1949). An admirable account of the theory of the passions on which Hume's moral theory is based is given in Páll S. Ardal's *Passion and Value in Hume's Treatise* (Edinburgh, 1966).

This book has another purpose as well. In the Notes and References in my *Ethics: Inventing Right and Wrong* (Penguin, 1977) I remarked that the best illustration and support for the view of ethics which I had presented in the first chapter of that book are provided by the works of some of the eighteenth-century British moralists. I am now developing that hint: I hope that my examination of the arguments of Hume and his predecessors and successors will serve, indirectly, as a further explanation and defence of several theses of my own.

I am very grateful to Michael Lockwood, Gene Mason, Roy Park, and Gerhard Streminger, all of whom read an earlier version of this book and whose comments have, I believe, helped me to improve it.

JLM

I

INTRODUCTION: OUTLINE OF HUME'S THEORY

Hume's ethical views are presented in his *Treatise*, the *Enquiry concerning the Principles of Morals*, and a number of essays; it is in the *Treatise* that we find the most interesting and provocative statement of them.[1] It occupies the whole of Book III, but the section in Book II entitled 'Of the influencing motives of the will' is also very important; it states his psychology of action, on which some of the main arguments at the beginning of Book III are based. We have, then, these divisions of his argument:

II iii 3:	Psychology of Action
III i 1–2:	Moral Epistemology
III ii 1–12:	The Artificial Virtues
III iii 1–5:	The Natural Virtues
III iii 6:	Conclusion

Hume's psychology of action is summed up in his dictum that reason is, and ought only to be, the slave of the passions. Less dramatically, his view is that all knowledge, whether of *a priori* truths or of empirical facts, all beliefs, and all rational calculation are by themselves inert. By themselves none of these things, which he includes under the heading of 'reason' in a broad sense, provides a motive for action, or for inaction either. None of these items, nor any collection of items from this list alone, can motivate anyone either to do anything or to refrain from doing anything. Motivation for or against any action requires something else, what he would call a passion or sentiment, and more particularly a desire. In conjunction with desires, of course, beliefs, knowledge, and calculation can help to determine what one does. Hume is not saying

1

(what would be most implausible) that 'reason' has no bearing at all on action. Indeed in the *Enquiry* he puts what is essentially the same view less provocatively by saying that '*reason* and *sentiment* concur in almost all moral determinations and conclusions' – that is, they co-operate to determine the judgments which issue in choice and action. In the *Treatise* he expresses it differently, since the original drive to action comes from some desire or passion or sentiment, he sees this as the governing element, with belief or knowledge or calculation playing a subordinate role, merely helping the desire to achieve satisfaction. He argues further that as reason cannot by itself supply any motive to action, equally it cannot by itself oppose any motive to action. No passion is, strictly speaking, contrary to reason. A passion can, however, if we speak less strictly, be called unreasonable in either of two senses: a passion may be based on the supposition of the existence of some object, and reason may discover that no such object exists, or reason may point out that a means chosen to secure the object of some passion is insufficient for that end.

In part i of Book III Hume argues that moral distinctions are not derived from reason and that they are derived from a moral sense. Hume's positive doctrine is open to several different interpretations in detail, and we shall have to consider (in chapter V) exactly how to understand it. But the broad outline of his view is that we call something virtuous if and because it produces in us a particular kind of pleasure, and we call something evil or vicious if and because it produces a particular kind of pain; the virtuousness or viciousness is not in the objects themselves, apart from the sentiments they provoke in us. We shall also find (in chapter IV) some indeterminacy in the negative part of Hume's doctrine, that moral distinctions are not derived from reason. But on the whole we can take him to be using 'reason' here in the broad sense which covers all knowledge, empirical as well as *a priori*, and all valid inference or calculation; if so, his doctrine means that moral distinctions do not report any objective features at all: moral goodness or rightness is not any quality or any relation to be found in or among objective situations or actions, and no purely intellectual or cognitive procedure can issue in a moral judgment. Hume's main argument for this negative thesis is based on his psychology of action. Reason alone, he has argued, cannot motivate to action or against action. But moral judgments do so motivate: the judgment that a certain proposed action would be right or good or virtuous influences the agent in favour of so acting – or at the least is intended to do so – and the judgment that it

2

would be wrong or evil or vicious similarly tends to deter him from so acting. Morality would be useless if it had no such direct influence on what people do. It follows at once that since morality does motivate and reason by itself does not motivate, morality cannot be a matter of reason alone. This is Hume's first and most important argument, but he backs it up with a number of others, and this section (III i 1) concludes with the famous passage in which he asks how an 'ought' can be derived from an 'is'.

The rest of Book III is devoted to a detailed account of just how various moral distinctions, in particular our recognition of certain character-traits or behavioural tendencies as virtues, are based on sentiments. But this account is both complicated and enriched by Hume's distinction between natural and artificial virtues. Hutcheson had argued that men have a natural tendency to benevolence; there is, he thought, an inborn tendency in human beings to desire the good of others, to want their fellow human beings to be happy rather than miserable. Equally naturally, because of a moral sense which God has implanted in us to direct our actions − analogous in some ways with the senses through which we perceive the material world − we tend to approve of actions in so far as they appear to express benevolence, and we call morally good whatever evokes this approval. Thus moral goodness is located in benevolence : morally good actions are benevolent ones, and the disposition to behave benevolently is the fundamental, if not the only, virtue. Now benevolence as Hutcheson saw it would be for Hume the paradigm of a natural virtue. It is natural in at least two ways. It is a tendency which human beings normally and naturally possess. Also it is naturally a virtue in that human beings tend naturally to approve of it. But Hume does not think that benevolence is the only natural virtue. He lists 'meekness, beneficence, charity, generosity, clemency, moderation, equity', also 'greatness of mind' and 'industry, perseverance, patience, activity, vigilance, application, constancy ... temperance, frugality, economy, resolution', and refers to prudence and courage and a due degree of pride, and is even inclined to include along with these such natural abilities as intelligence and wit and eloquence. Some of these are closely related to benevolence, but many others are not, and are directly beneficial primarily to the person who has them. Hume in fact classifies as virtues any mental qualities that are either immediately agreeable or useful either to their possessor or to others. But a large number of these are dispositions which people both naturally have in some degree and naturally approve of. Also, it is fairly easy to understand why people have these dispositions and why they approve of them. We might regard both the approval tendency and the dispositions as having been put into us by a God who is himself benevolent and who has planned human nature so that men can flourish in ordinary conditions on earth and can live fairly happily in society with one another: this is how Hutcheson saw them. Alternatively, we might accept them just as familiar contingent facts which at least fit in with other aspects of human nature, which may well be direct, or not very indirect, expressions of instincts which it is plausible to suppose men to have. These natural virtues are therefore not puzzling from a moral sense point of view, though Hume offers fairly complicated psychological explanations of why we approve or disapprove of dispositions just as we do. But there are other dispositions and patterns of behaviour which are commonly regarded as virtuous, but which are at first sight much more puzzling: for example, the respect for all the rules about private property. Why should people have property rights, and why should others have any inclination to respect them? Whence comes the motive for the sort of honesty that is displayed in not helping oneself to what is said to belong to someone else? Why do people generally approve of such honesty and disapprove so strongly of dishonesty? Again, what is the motive for keeping contracts and promises and agreements, and why do we approve of this sort of fidelity and disapprove of those who break their agreements? How do we even get the notion of an agreement or a promise in the first place? Again, why do people obey and support the rulers or governments of their countries, and why is it thought right to do so (even when a ruler demands that one should do something that would not otherwise be thought right), and wrong to engage in what is called treason or rebellion? Again, why (in Hume's time, if not today) were chastity and modesty regarded as virtues in women? Of all these supposed virtues, none is obviously or directly comprehensible either as an instinctive disposition or as an object of general approval and admiration in the way that benevolence, for example, is, or prudence or industry. If we have a moral sense which favours honesty and promise-keeping and loyalty to rulers and female chastity – and not only these as broad tendencies but all the complicated rules which these terms cover – then it calls for some further explanation. Yet it is no good going back to talk about reason requiring any of these forms of conduct. Even apart from Hume's general proof that nothing which comes under the heading of reason can by itself be the motive for any action, or can supply any independent directive, it is not possible to make out a specific rational

4

case in favour of any one of these curious behaviour patterns. (It may seem obvious, indeed tautologous, that one ought not to take what belongs to someone else without his permission; but this means only that the puzzling rule has been built into the way in which we speak about possessions. Sort out the synthetic rule which is implicit in our terminology, for example, that you ought not to take from someone something given to him by his rich uncle, and you will not find any rational necessity in it.) Hume's solution to the puzzle is that these are artificial virtues: both the tendency to act in each of these ways and the tendency to approve of such actions can be seen as inventions, artificial devices which have somehow been added to whatever tendencies to action men instinctively possessed and whatever instinctive moral sense they originally had. Both the behavioural tendencies and the approval tendencies which support them are indeed useful; they fulfil certain social functions, they help human society to flourish, and this fact somehow explains why they are there.

The main themes of Book III, part ii, then, are, first, arguments to show that these things are, in Hume's sense, artificial virtues, and, secondly, attempts to explain in what way they are useful and how they could have and presumably have grown up.

In Book III, part iii, Hume turns to the natural virtues, having rather oddly dealt first with those aspects of morality which are the more puzzling from his general point of view, and only later coming to more straightforward matters. Here his main interest is in tracing the various natural virtues and, in particular, the sentiment of approval of them, to their origin in a basic human tendency which he calls *sympathy*, an inclination to share (what one believes to be) the feelings of others. Whereas Hume's explanation of the artificial virtues is essentially sociological, his explanation of the natural virtues is essentially psychological. But, having developed this account, he concludes by arguing that the artificial virtues also are approved of – and so count as virtues – only through the operation of sympathy, which thus becomes the foundation of his whole moral theory. He thinks it should be a welcome conclusion that morality has such an attractive basis.

As this brief survey shows, Hume's moral theory is not primarily an attempt to answer the first order practical question, 'What ought we to do?' He is not asserting particular obligations or duties, nor putting forward a general normative doctrine like utilitarianism. Nor, on the whole, is he recommending particular dispositions as virtues, saying that such and such ways of behaving *are* virtuous, and such and such

5

contrary ones vicious. But equally Hume is not primarily concerned to answer such second order, conceptual, questions as have played so large a part in recent moral philosophy, such as 'What do our moral judgments mean?', or 'How are they to be analysed?', or 'What logical constraints do they obey?' Rather, his question is a demand for an explanation of the sort typically given by the empirical sciences: 'Here is this curious phenomenon, human morality, a cluster of attitudes, dispositions, practices, behavioural tendencies, and so on that we find almost universally among men, even in different societies and at different times: why is it there, and how did it develop?' This is a question that might, perhaps, have been answered (and would have been answered by many of Hume's contemporaries and predecessors) by postulating innate moral ideas and faculties, implanted in human beings by their creator; but that is not Hume's approach. Alternatively, it may be answered in sociological and psychological terms, by constructing and defending a causal hypothesis; this is what Hume has done. It is not for nothing that his work is entitled *A Treatise of Human Nature*, and sub-titled *An attempt to introduce the experimental method of reasoning into moral subjects*; it is an attempt to study and explain moral phenomena (as well as human knowledge and emotions) in the same sort of way in which Newton and his followers studied and explained the physical world.[2]

II

SOME PREDECESSORS: HOBBES, SHAFTESBURY, CLARKE, WOLLASTON, MANDEVILLE, HUTCHESON, BUTLER

We can take Thomas Hobbes as the first speaker in a sustained philosophical debate that extends over more than a hundred years and that culminates in, but does not end with, Hume's moral theory.[1] Many able thinkers, though disagreeing widely with one another, were all concerned to find an answer to Hobbes. But perhaps it will turn out that, though he was certainly wrong on some points, on others – including perhaps the most vital ones – Hobbes was essentially right, and the conclusion to be drawn from the long debate is only a revised version of the challenge that started it.

Hobbes's general metaphysical theory is materialist: everything in the world, including human beings and their minds, is to be explained ultimately in terms of matter in motion. Men have desires and aversions, but their motives are entirely selfish. 'Good' and 'evil' are words which express only the relation of things to the speaker's desires.

> Whatsoever is the object of any man's appetite or desire; that is it which he for his part calleth *good*: and the object of his hate, and aversion, *evil*; and of his contempt, *vile* and *inconsiderable*. For these words of good, evil, and contemptible, are ever used with relation to the person that useth them: there being nothing simply and absolutely so; nor any common rule of good and evil, to be taken from the nature of the objects themselves ...(25).[2]

There is no room for objective moral qualities or relations in this strictly materialist universe. But on this foundation Hobbes builds a social and political theory.

Being naturally purely selfish, men come into conflict with one

7

another. In the first place, 'if any two men desire the same thing, which nevertheless they cannot both enjoy, they become enemies', and so each tries to destroy or subdue the other. But knowing that this may happen, each fears any other who may compete with him, and conflicts arise secondly from this distrust: each tries to get his blow in first. Thirdly, since to be thought powerful is itself a source of power, men fight to maintain their reputations. Thus Hobbes finds three principal causes of quarrel: competition, diffidence, and glory. He adds that men are naturally not so unequal in strength as to set up any stable chain of subordination, any 'pecking order'. A weak man can kill the strongest by some sort of trickery, or at any rate two or three weak men can kill a strong man whom they all fear. Consequently, Hobbes concludes that the natural state of men is a war of all against all, with the result that there is no society, no security, no industry, no cultivation of the soil, no civilization, no technical progress; men live in continual fear and danger of violent death, and, in the most memorable of Hobbes's many memorable phrases, the life of man is 'solitary, poor, nasty, brutish, and short'. In this state of nature, nothing is wrong. No one has any obligation to help or respect others. Hobbes says that everyone has a right to all things, but this means only that there is nothing that it would be wrong for him to take if he wanted it: there are as yet no moral principles or constraints at all.

Yet men have both the appropriate desires and enough intelligence to get them out of this deplorable condition. Above all each man desires his own survival, and he has the wit to see that the best chance of this would lie in the establishing of a state of peace rather than war. So it is a 'precept, or general rule of reason, *That every man, ought to endeavour peace, as far as he has hope of obtaining it* ...' (57). But since this is simply a counsel of prudence, in Kant's terms a hypothetical imperative which presents itself to everyone just because he wants to preserve his own life, Hobbes adds the rider, '*and when he cannot obtain it, that he may seek, and use, all helps, and advantages of war*'. Thus we have the double-barrelled rule, '*seek peace, and follow it*', but also '*By all means we can ... defend ourselves*'. Hobbes calls the first part of this the first law of nature. From it he derives a second law:

That a man be willing, when others are so too, as far-forth, as for peace, and defence of himself he shall think it necessary, to lay down this right to all things; and to be contented with so much liberty against other men as he would allow other men against himself.

8

This second law means that it is reasonable for men, still for purely selfish reasons, to make some kind of non-aggression pact with one another. After explaining at some length what an agreement or covenant is, Hobbes derives from his second law a third, *'That men perform their covenants made'*, in other words, that if you make an agreement you should keep it. And he goes on in the same spirit to formulate altogether sixteen 'laws of nature' (57–74).

Hobbes's terminology might suggest that he is, after all, smuggling in a set of objective moral rules. He says that the science of these laws of nature is the only true moral philosophy, that is, the science of what is good and evil 'in the conversation, and society of mankind'. But there is no inconsistency here. He explains carefully that these are only 'theorems concerning what conduceth to the conservation and defence of themselves'; that is, they are essentially causal statements about what will bring it about that men will, or will not, survive, which can be true in a thoroughly objective way. They can also be construed as hypothetical imperatives, which look at these causal relations from the point of view of their possible means-end use. As hypothetical imperatives, they belong to the sub-class which Kant called assertoric. Their general form is 'If you are to preserve your own life, you ought to do such and such; and you do very much want to preserve your own life.' Hobbes is saying that the necessary means to self-preservation are, in order, the readiness to seek peace, willingness to make non-aggression pacts, the keeping of agreements when you have made them, and thirteen further related principles of behaviour that will help to maintain peace or to restore it after a temporary breakdown.

But there is another important twist to the argument. Since these laws are hypothetical imperatives, they prescribe peace-seeking and non-aggression pacts and agreement-keeping and the rest only as means to an end, and therefore only if they will work; that is, only if others will do the same towards you. I should not be preserving myself, but quite the reverse, if I disarmed unilaterally, or even if I failed to take every advantage open to me, unless I had a firm assurance that others would not take advantage of my mildness. And what assurance could I have of this in the state of nature? Even if an agreement were made, what assurance could I have that it would be kept? It looks as if, starting from the war of all against all, everyone would have the intelligence to see that it would be to everyone's advantage if they all made and then kept an agreement to stop fighting and somehow divide and share the goods over which disputes arise, and yet no such agreement could ever come into

9

force because no one could trust others to keep it, partly because those others in turn could not trust anyone else (77, 79).

Hobbes had in fact discovered a paradigm case of what is now known as the Prisoners' Dilemma, a situation where everyone would be better off if they were to co-operate, but each, as a rationally selfish individual, will do better for himself if he does not co-operate, whether the others do so or not; so in fact they will not co-operate, and will all be worse off than if they did. In such a situation making an agreement to co-operate does not in itself help, because even after making it each has the same motive for breaking it that he originally had for not co-operating.

It might be objected that if each person's co-operation would encourage the others to co-operate, it would be to each person's interest to keep the agreement, because the immediate advantage he would gain by breaking it would be outweighed by the loss he would suffer when others followed his example. Consequently, it might be to each man's advantage, if all the others were willing to co-operate, to co-operate also, rather than to try to take advantage of their non-aggression; but how can each be sufficiently sure that the others will co-operate to be able to take the risk of being peaceable himself? How is he to know, starting from the state of war, that his own co-operation would encourage the others to co-operate? Hobbes often writes as if he had this form of the problem in mind; this is not a pure Prisoners' Dilemma, but it is close to one.

Hobbes does not conclude, however, that men cannot get out of the state of war, but rather that if they are to do this a further move is needed. They must set up a 'common power' to enforce their peace-making agreement; only where there is such a common power will they be able to trust one another. Therefore the only viable agreement that can be made in the state of nature, and therefore the one which it is reasonable for everyone, still for purely selfish motives, to make, is one which provides for its own enforcement. The first and fundamental agreement must be to set up and obey a political sovereign, that is, one man or some body of men that has the primary function of punishing anyone who fails to keep the non-aggression pact. By this device the situation is radically altered. If any considerable proportion of people obey the sovereign, he will have the power to punish deviators, and he will have the will to do so, because this will tend to maintain his own advantageous position. So anyone who thinks of breaking the agreement can calculate that he is unlikely to get away with it – if he does so at all, it can only be because the others fail to detect his delinquency, and it is not

10

reasonable to rely on their continuing to make such a mistake – so for purely selfish reasons he will keep the agreement after all. The situation has been miraculously transformed from a Prisoners' Dilemma, or something like one, to one where there is a stable equilibrium of peace-keeping: each subject, and the sovereign too, will now play his part because it is in his own interest to do so, and it will be in his interest because he knows that everyone else will be playing his part for the same reason. At any rate, that is what would happen if everyone were rational, still in a purely selfish way. Hobbes thinks that most people will be rationally and so now beneficially selfish if they listen to his arguments and are not led astray by mischievous religious and political teachings which would undermine their acceptance of established political authority – for example, the doctrines that the sovereign has only limited power, and is subject to the civil law, that liberty against the sovereign is a good thing, that people have absolute rights to property, which the sovereign cannot override, so that taxation requires the consent of the governed, that every man is the judge of good and evil actions, that it is a sin to act against your conscience, that spiritual wisdom is acquired by inspiration, and that a church may be independent of the government and have a separate claim to the obedience of its members (64, 81).[3]

In this way, then, the state of nature is replaced by that of civil society. When this is achieved, people have the security that makes possible industry and the prosperity which it can produce. So now all sixteen of the laws of nature are actually in force in the sense that it is in everyone's selfish interest to obey them, partly because they are likely to be enforced against anyone who was inclined to break them, but also because obedience to them is now the best means available of maintaining civil society, of preventing a lapse back into the state of war, and so of providing the best chance of one's own preservation.

It is no reply to Hobbes merely to point out that his state of nature and original social contract are unhistorical fictions. He is quite willing to concede this. What matters for him is that there are forces in human nature which would produce a war of all against all if it were not for the political structure of civil society, and which tend to be released, and to push us in that direction, whenever the power or authority of a government is undermined by internal dissension or rebellion or civil war. Nor is it a serious criticism to point out that men are not completely selfish, that there is enough instinctive affection to unite, for example, small family groups; a war of every small group against every other

11

small group would be almost as destructive as what was literally a war of all against all. There are, however, some real objections to his views, for example to his belief that any limitation or division of the sovereign's power would set the stage for a civil war. Some of these objections will emerge later. For the present I want rather to stress the general character of Hobbes's theory. It is an elaborate and ingenious attempt to construct a system of morality on a thoroughgoing materialist basis and on the assumption of purely selfish motives, which will yet show that people have reasons for acting in what are essentially the ways that traditional moral precepts demand, but which includes an absolute political sovereign as an allegedly vital element.

There are, indeed, other aspects of Hobbes's thought. He does speak of the laws of nature as being also commands of God, and as being, on that account, laws in the strict sense, not mere theorems about the means to survival and prosperity (77). It is not clear whether he means that this would make them into categorical imperatives, or merely into still more forceful hypothetical imperatives with divine rewards and punishments as additional sanctions. He also devotes a large part of *Leviathan* to interpreting the Bible so that it supports his political contentions, and cannot be used to justify religious organizations in resisting or rebelling against the authority of the state. But though this side of his writing was highly relevant in his own time, it is much less important now.[4] For us, and even for his eighteenth-century successors, the most interesting line of thought in *Leviathan* is the one I have sketched. One other influential and provocative part of Hobbes's thought, closely related to his materialism, in his energetic assertion and defence of strict causal determinism: every event, including every human action, is determined by antecedent causes. Actions can be free only in the sense that they may result from the agent's will, but that will itself is determined by earlier causes. Liberty is '*the absence of all the impediments to action that are not contained in the nature and intrinsical quality of the agent*', and events are called contingent only when we do not perceive and do not know their causes (95–6).

As I have said, several moral philosophers in the next hundred years were concerned to answer Hobbes, and not merely to refute his political absolutism, but still more to attack the basic principles from which he derived it. Thus Samuel Clarke sets out to oppose Hobbes's doctrines

that there is no such thing as just and unjust, right and wrong originally in the nature of things, that men in their natural state ... are

12

not obliged to universal benevolence, nor to any moral duty whatever
… and that, in civil societies, it depends wholly upon positive laws or
the will of governors, to define what shall be just or unjust (252).

Shaftesbury claims that men naturally have 'public affections', which
tend towards the good of the society to which they belong, or, indeed,
that of the whole human species, as well as private affections that tend
towards the individual's own good. Hutcheson also holds that
benevolence is a natural and universal characteristic of men, and that
there is no need to explain away what appears to be benevolence as an
indirect result of self-love. Butler insists on the reality, as parts of human
nature, along with self-love, not only of benevolence but also of a
conscience which prescribes morally right actions and of various
particular passions which have to be distinguished from self-love. He
argues against Hobbes that self-love not merely is not but even could not
be the sole human motive. Butler agrees with Clarke that there are
objective moral relations, that 'vice is contrary to the nature and reason
of things'; but he also holds that we can base morality on human nature,
but that if we do so properly we arrive at somewhat different
conclusions from those of Hobbes, and by a very different route.
Mandeville, on the other hand, agrees with Hobbes that man is not a
naturally social animal, but goes beyond him in describing morality as a
deliberate invention. Hume himself is in an equivocal position. He comes
close to Hobbes in his account of the artificial virtues; yet he claims to
base his whole moral theory on sympathy − an instinctive tendency to
share the feelings of others − and sympathy can easily generate
benevolence.

Anthony Ashley Cooper, the third Earl of Shaftesbury, sees the whole
world as a predominantly harmonious system. There are parts which
make up wholes, which are in turn parts of larger wholes, and so on.
Each part has its own good, but it also contributes to the good of the
whole of which it is a part. Among animals, male and female have a
relation to one another: they are designed to fit together. But, also, male
and female together 'have a joint relation to another existence': they are
designed to produce offspring and to perpetuate the race or species of
which they are members. But a whole species of animals may contribute
to the well-being of another species − most obviously by being part of the
latter's food supply − so that the former species as a whole is only a part
of a larger system (197). Shaftesbury's explanation of morality is then
simple. Human beings have passions which benefit the species to which

13

they belong, '*natural affection*, parental kindness, zeal for posterity, concern for the propagation and nurture of the young, love of fellowship and company, compassion, mutual succour, and the rest of this kind'. Given that a creature has these tendencies, you need only provide it also with 'a reflective faculty', and it will also approve of these tendencies; that is, it will '*be capable of virtue, and have a sense of right and wrong*' (204–5). The moral sense is simply a self-conscious form of the social affections.

Shaftesbury also admits, however, that human beings have private affections which tend towards the good of the individual, the 'self-system', as well as the public affections which tend towards the good of the 'system of the kind'; they may, indeed, also have unnatural affections, which tend neither towards the good of the kind nor towards that of the individual. But then, if private and public good conflict, will it not be irrational to sacrifice self-interest to the good of the species?

Shaftesbury grants that either the public or the private affections may, in a given individual, be either too strong or too weak. But he professes to prove that 'to have the natural, kindly, or generous affections strong and powerful towards the good of the public, is to have the chief means and power of self-enjoyment', and that to lack them is certain misery, and again that 'to have the private or self-affections too strong, or beyond their degree of subordinacy to the kindly and natural, is also miserable', and, of course, that to have the unnatural affections is to be miserable in the highest degree (206–7, 214).

It would follow that there is a natural harmony between self-interest and public interest, and consequently a natural society among human beings, and that there is no need for Hobbes's elaborate construction of an artificial political society on the basis of self-interest and naturally unrestrained competition.

However, it is easy to see that Shaftesbury is much too optimistic. Parental affection and care are, no doubt, natural in humans as in other animals; but they tend towards the preservation of each individual's own descendants – strictly, towards the survival and multiplication of his own genes – not towards the good of his species.[5] It is a further confusion to identify either the preservation of one's own genes or the survival of the species with the well-being of a society. Most of the other facts to which Shaftesbury draws attention show only that an individual needs, in order to flourish, friendly relationships with some small number of other people. This does nothing to restrain the tendency of each such group to compete with other groups, or to resolve each

14

individual's conflicts with individuals not in his immediate circle. At most, Shaftesbury shows that Hobbes has slightly mis-stated the problem. As Hume rightly puts it, what produces competition is not pure selfishness, but a combination of selfishness with 'confined generosity'. Shaftesbury's explanation of the moral sense is also inadequate. A self-conscious form of the social affections would be just that, and no more; but the moral sense is something more. It ranges more widely than the social affections, suggesting that we have obligations towards people whom we have no immediate inclination to love or help or respect. It prescribes conformity to universal rules or principles of conduct. It suggests that there are things that we must do, and others that we must not do, no matter how we feel about them. And we make moral comments on the actions and characters of people who are remote from us and, so far as any literal affections are concerned, indifferent to us. Something further, then, is needed to explain morality; either a considerable elaboration of Shaftesbury's account, or some quite different one.[6]

Samuel Clarke's account is quite different; whereas Shaftesbury represents the moral sense school, Clarke represents the rationalists. There are, he holds, 'necessary and eternal *different relations*, that different things bear one to another', and a consequent '*fitness or unfitness* of the application of different things or different relations one to another'.

> … these eternal and necessary differences of things make it *fit and reasonable* for creatures so to act; they cause it to be their *duty*, or lay an *obligation* upon them, so to do; even separate from the consideration of these rules being the *positive will* or *command of God*; and also antecedently to any respect or regard, expectation or apprehension, *of any particular private and personal advantage or disadvantage, reward or punishment*, either present or future; annexed either by natural consequence, or by positive appointment, to the practising or neglecting of these rules (225).

In other words, there are objective duties and obligations, arising directly out of the nature of things, prior to and independent of the will of God – let alone that of any human or political authority – and not derived in any way from self-interest – neither from any naturally beneficial results of right action or naturally bad results of wrong action for the agent, nor from any humanly or divinely instituted rewards or punishments either in this world or in the next. And the connection between any particular

15

sort of action which is obligatory and its being obligatory, its being intrinsically required of us, is not due to any contingent affection or sense, but is necessary, eternal, immutable, and rationally knowable as such.

This is as complete and uncompromising a statement of moral objectivism as one could possibly desire. It is totally opposed to Hobbes's view that morality is merely the best means to self-preservation for incorrigibly selfish and naturally competitive creatures. But it is almost equally opposed to Shaftesbury's thesis that morality rests upon or consists in the contingent empirical facts that human beings have public affections and will be happiest when these are well developed and dominant in them. Again, it is in radical conflict with the sort of theological ethics which sees morality as created by or resting upon the positive commands of God – a view adopted in some places by Hobbes, but also by many other thinkers. For Clarke, morality is logically prior to God's will; since God is himself good, his will conforms to what is already, independently, morally right, and could not make something morally right or wrong which was not already so. Speaking loosely, we might perhaps say that a particular kind of action becomes right or obligatory through being commanded by God, though it would otherwise be indifferent; but strictly speaking it is not this particular kind of action that is then right, but rather obedience to God; and that was right already. This general form of action, obeying whatever God requires, is eternally and immutably obligatory; it is not God's commands that make it our duty to obey God's commands.

This last point is made most clearly by another of the rationalists, Cudworth.

But if we would speak yet more accurately and precisely, we might rather say, that no positive commands whatsoever do make anything morally good and evil, just and unjust, which nature had not made such before. For indifferent things commanded, considered materially in themselves, remain still what they were before in their own nature, that is, indifferent, because (as Aristotle speaks) will cannot change nature. And those things that are by nature indifferent, must needs be immutably so, as those things that are by nature just or unjust, honest or shameful. But all the moral goodness, justice and virtue that is exercised in obeying positive commands, and doing such things as are positive only and to be done for no other cause but because they are commanded, or in respect to political order, consisteth not in the

16

materiality of the actions themselves, but in that formality of yielding obedience to the commands of lawful authority in them. Just as when a man covenanteth or promiseth to do an indifferent thing which by natural justice he was not bound to do, the virtue of doing it consisteth not in the materiality of the action promised, but in the formality of keeping faith and performing covenants. Wherefore in positive commands, the will of the commander doth not create any new moral entity, but only diversly modifies and determines that general duty or obligation of natural justice to obey lawful authority and keep oaths and covenants, as our own will in promising doth but produce several modifications of keeping faith. And therefore there are no new things just or due made by either of them, besides what was always by nature such, to keep our own promises, and obey the lawful commands of others (125).

Against the view that morality is created by God's commands, Clarke and Cudworth have a strong case. If duties were constituted by commands, so that something's being obligatory just was its being commanded, the devil's commands would constitute duties too. If the duty to obey God's commands rested (as Hobbes says) simply on his power to reward and punish, then if the devil were omnipotent it would be our duty to obey him. Since neither conclusion is acceptable to the theological moralist, he must say that the duty to obey God's commands is derived either from his goodness or from his having, antecedently, the right to command, and so in either case from moral principles which are themselves prior to the commands of God, not created by them.

But though he has a strong case against theological ethics of this sort, Clarke has much less of a case for his own view. Compared with the admirable forthrightness of his assertions, Clarke's arguments are disappointing. They are little more than an appeal to self-evidence, with the suggestion that the necessity of moral truths is analogous to that of mathematical propositions. Moral fitnesses are said to be as undeniable as relations of proportion in arithmetic (e.g., $12:8::9:6$) or the congruence of figures in geometry. Because God is infinitely superior to men, it is fit that they should honour, worship, obey and imitate him. It is necessarily fitter that God, as author and creator of the universe, should govern all things to constant and regular ends, than that everything should be left to chance, and it is necessarily fitter that the all-powerful governor of the world should do what tends most to the universal good of the whole creation than that he should make the

17

whole continually miserable; it is fit, in particular, that he should make good men happy. Likewise, 'it is undeniably more fit, absolutely and in the nature of the thing itself, that all men should endeavour to promote the universal good and welfare of all; than that men should be continually contriving the ruin and destruction of all' (226).

Clarke thinks that pretty well everyone will agree with him.

These things are so notoriously plain and self-evident that nothing but the extremest stupidity of mind, corruption of manners, or perverseness of spirit, can possibly make any man entertain the least doubt concerning them. For a man endued with reason, to deny the truth of these things; is the very same thing, as if a man that has the use of his sight, should at the same time that he beholds the sun, deny that there is any such thing as light in the world; or as if a man that understands geometry or arithmetic, should deny the most obvious and known proportions of lines or numbers, and perversely contend that the whole is not equal to all its parts, or that a square is not double to a triangle of equal base and height ... (227).

But to prick this balloon of rhetoric it is only necessary for someone to say firmly, 'But the cases you are comparing are not alike: the alleged moral proportionality between actions and situations is not evident in the same way as proportions between lines or numbers'. and to challenge Clarke and his followers to produce a moral demonstration that is cogent in the same way as one in geometry or arithmetic. This is just what Hume did when he said, in a deliberately provocative way, ' 'Tis not contrary to reason to prefer the destruction of the whole world to the scratching of my finger. 'Tis not contrary to reason for me to chuse my total ruin, to prevent the least uneasiness of an *Indian* or person wholly unknown to me' (*Treatise* II iii 3). But it was necessary for someone to say this. Clarke and writers like him – and they are still to be found today – will get away with their unsubstantiated rhetoric unless they are challenged, and challenged repeatedly. Clarke does, indeed, try to do better than this, and to criticize Hobbes by finding inconsistencies within his system. But I think that a careful reading will show that he cannot find any real inconsistencies in Hobbes's argument, and that even here Clarke is constantly relying on appeals to self-evidence.

But do these appeals have some force? Clarke can show that we all have some tendency to prefer, other things being equal, to act in ways that moral principles require; that 'there is hardly any wicked man, but

18

when his own case is represented to him under the person of another, will freely enough pass sentence against the wickedness he himself is guilty of'; that we are very ready to 'cry out for equity, and exclaim against injustice' when we are the victims of violence or fraud; that in learning of actions remote from us in time or place, where our own interests are not involved, we tend to approve of the kinds of actions that are commonly regarded as morally right and to disapprove of those commonly regarded as morally wrong; and also that we have some tendency to see moral requirements as absolute, non-contingent, and not derived from self-interest (233, 236–7).

There is, then, some truth in Clarke's claim that 'the mind of man cannot avoid giving its assent to the eternal law of righteousness.' We seem to see requirements to act or not to act in certain ways as arising directly out of the hard facts of the situations in question, as directly supervenient upon the natural features of those situations and the proposed actions. But this falls far short of a *demonstration* of these requirements as necessary consequences of those natural features. It looks as if the moral objectivist has to give up the claim that it is *reason* (in any sense analogous to that in which reason operates in mathematics) that supplies moral knowledge, and fall back rather on the claim that what we have here is an *intuition*, a direct perception of a necessary truth, not open to further defence or explanation. This is explicitly admitted by later 'rationalists'; Richard Price speaks of our having 'a power of immediately perceiving right and wrong', and Thomas Reid says that 'all moral reasonings rest upon one or more first principles of morals, whose truth is immediately perceived without reasoning, by all men come to years of understanding' (672–3, 879, and Reid's *Essays on the Active Powers of Man*, Essay III, part iii, chapter 6).

But how would Hobbes, for example, or Shaftesbury respond to the correct point that Clarke is here making? Hobbes would presumably say that most of us have become so accustomed to acting in accordance with the theorems which point out the best means to self-preservation, and to encouraging these ways of behaving in others, that we have forgotten their original purpose, and mistakenly see them as immediate requirements of the situations themselves. But then he is open to this objection may not these moral beliefs, whatever their origin, take over the task of making men social, and so render the device of political sovereignty unnecessary? May not man, by virtue of these beliefs, have become a social animal after all, even if he was not one to start with? To this Hobbes would surely reply that these moral beliefs are too weak to do this job on their own. After all, to reveal them Clarke has had to turn to situations where our self-interest is somehow either suspended or else engaged on the same side as moral belief. This suggests that moral belief is only a fairly weak motive in most people, easily submerged beneath self-interest, and therefore not powerful enough to resolve the conflicts which arise from self-interested competition. If so, then Hobbes's political structure may be needed after all.

Shaftesbury, on the other hand, would welcome the evidence which Clarke assembles, but interpret it as showing not that men have a rational or even an intuitive knowledge of an objective moral law, but only that they have public affections and are self-consciously aware of them. But, as I have said, this would not adequately explain why we seem to find moral requirements in cases where our affections are not engaged, or why they seem authoritative for us and external to us. We should need to add something to Shaftesbury's account before it could explain the phenomenon of moral belief.

William Wollaston is another thinker in the rationalist tradition. His views are close to those of Clarke. But Wollaston tries to give – as Clarke so obviously failed to give – a general characterization of all morally wrong acts and, based on that, a demonstration of their wrongness.

Wollaston starts by defining truth, and defining it correctly:[7] *'Those propositions are true, which express things as they are: or, truth is the conformity of those words or signs, by which things are expressed, to the things themselves'* (274).

Next he makes the interesting suggestion that a proposition may be denied, or asserted, by actions rather than by words. This is as it were an inverse of Austin's theory of performative utterances.[8] Whereas Austin holds that you can do things with words, Wollaston holds that you can say things with actions. He does not mean merely that gestures can replace or supplement speech. That is a minor point. Wollaston uses rather this example: 'If a body of soldiers, seeing another body approach, should fire upon them, would not this action declare that they were enemies …?' – and, of course, if the second body were not enemies of the first, this declaration would be false. We cannot brush this aside by saying that those who fired on their friends were just making a mistake. If their officer had explicitly said 'Those are enemies', he would have again been making a mistake, but for all that he would have said something false. So when the first body fires, though they are indeed making a mistake, this does not prevent them from also, by their action, declaring something false (275–6).

20

Similarly, if someone makes a promise, and then fails to fulfil it when the time comes, he declares, and declares falsely, by his action that he never made such a promise. Again, by the way I use or dispose of certain goods I may in effect declare that they belong to me (277).

Wollaston notes that actions may have a significance attached to them by convention, as words always do. Christians take their hats off when they pray; Jews put their hats on. So the act of taking off one's hat, which signifies reverence among Christians, would signify irreverence among Jews. But both these meanings are purely conventional; taking off one's hat, as such, has no natural meaning. But this differs from the case where my using goods in a certain way signifies that they belong to me: here the significance is natural, not conventional, and could not differ from one community to another. Where these natural meanings are concerned, actions express propositions more strongly than words themselves, for the meaning of words is always conventional. Thus 'whoever acts as if things were so, or not so, doth by his acts declare that they are so, or not so'; as plainly as he could by words, and with more reality' (279).

With these preliminaries, Wollaston can state his basic general principle of morality: '*No act* (whether word or deed) *of any being to whom moral good and evil are imputable*' — that is, of any responsible free agent — '*that interferes with any true proposition, or denies any thing to be as it is, can be right*' (280).

If Wollaston's argument were to go through, it would have obvious merits. It would give us a single unifying principle governing the distinction between right and wrong in all cases. It would be a rule of action, such as Hobbes had denied there to be, taken directly from the nature of the objects themselves. While cognitivists and non-cognitivists dispute about whether moral judgments and principles are capable of being true or false, Wollaston carries the battle right into the non-cognitivist camp by arguing that the rightness of actions just is truth and that their wrongness just is falsity. If a morally characterizable act just is the expression of a true or false proposition, then of course the judgment that this act is right or wrong, that is, true or false, will itself be either true or false. And Wollaston has no difficulty in showing that his theory fits in nicely with such widely held doctrines as that to act rightly is to do what is in accordance with nature, or with reason, or with the will of God, and that to act wrongly is to go against each of these.

This is, then, an ingenious and attractive theory. But it is open to two fundamental objections. One concerns the prescriptive force of moral

21

judgments. The problem for a rationalist, as we have seen with Clarke, is to show how a directive to action necessarily and rationally supervenes upon the hard facts of a situation. But Wollaston's theory does little to solve this problem. Suppose that the moralist could say, of a proposed action, 'That would express a falsehood, that would deny that things are as they are', the agent might well reply 'So what?', and go ahead and express the falsehood all the same. Bertrand Russell defined a pedant as a man who likes his statements to be true, and no doubt we are all at least mildly pedantic in this sense; but only mildly. Knowing that a statement – or, in Wollaston's theory, an action – would express a falsehood does not give me a very strong motive for refraining from it. The rationalist's programme is to show that there are objectively valid necessary principles of *action*, intrinsically authoritative *prescriptions* or *directives*. Even if his proposal went through and were open to no other objections, Wollaston would have achieved the objective validity only at the price of doing away with the prescriptivity, or greatly weakening it.

But in any case there is a second objection, which comes to light when Wollaston tries to show how his theory yields specific rules for action. How does my riding off on someone else's horse without his permission express a falsehood, deny that the horse belongs to this other man? In the first place my act expresses and fulfils the prescription 'Let me ride off on this horse without X's permission.' This can be a falsehood, or deny that things are as they are, only if the way things are includes a contrary prescription 'Don't ride off on this horse without X's permission'; and, of course, the proposition that this horse *belongs* to X, that is, that X has a certain cluster of rights with regard to this horse, implicitly includes this prescription. But this means that we can find a falsehood expressed by my act only if we *assume* that X has this cluster of rights; in other words we have to *presuppose* the relevant moral principles. To take another of Wollaston's examples: if I, being reasonably well off, were never to give anything in charity to the poor, I should thereby deny that the condition of the poor is what it is or that my situation is what it is. But this presupposes that our contrasting economic positions give the poor some general claim on me: it is only in the light of such a presupposition that my failure to be charitable denies that things are as they really are. All the work, we may say, is being done in each case by moral prescriptions which Wollaston is simply presupposing. He does not, therefore, succeed in deriving moral rules or judgments from the principle 'That every intelligent, active, and free being should ... treat every thing as being what it is' alone; rather he has surreptitiously to include moral requirements in his view of the way things antecedently are.

Another writer of this period is Bernard Mandeville. Unlike Shaftesbury, Clarke, and Wollaston, he is close in spirit to Hobbes; but his views are even more cynical than those of Hobbes. Two of his doctrines are particularly worthy of record. One is summed up in the sub-title of his *Fable of the Bees*: 'Private Vices, Public Benefits'. Anticipating the *laissez-faire* economists (whom he probably influenced) he argued that if people selfishly pursue luxury, they will unintentionally benefit one another and promote general prosperity, whereas if each practised the self-denial that moralists are continually preaching the result would be that everyone would be much worse off. Another view, equally cynical but not easily reconciled with the former, is put forward in his *Enquiry into the Origin of Moral Virtue*. Like Hobbes, Mandeville says that man is not a naturally sociable animal; in fact, 'no species of animals is, without the curb of government, less capable of agreeing long together in multitudes than that of man'; also, 'being an extraordinary selfish and headstrong, as well as cunning animal, however he may be subdued by superior strength, it is impossible by force alone to make him tractable ...' (263). You can't keep a bad man down.

Consequently 'lawgivers and other wise men, that have laboured for the establishment of society', have tried to make people believe that it would benefit each person to conquer rather than to indulge his appetites, and to care for the public interest rather than what seems to be his private interest. But it is not easy to make people believe this. So, being unable to give them real rewards for public-spirited actions, they contrived an imaginary reward for self-denial, a reward which cost nobody anything, but which was yet a most acceptable recompense to those who received it. This was praise and flattery. These wise men realized that all human beings are extremely susceptible to flattery, and by praising public-spirited actions as noble and rational, and condemning purely selfish ones as bestial and sub-human, they persuaded people to control their selfish tendencies for the general benefit of their fellows. In particular, they drew a contrast between two types of men: the first, abject, low-minded people, who are always hunting after immediate enjoyment, incapable of self-denial, with no regard to the good of others; the second, lofty, high-spirited creatures, free from sordid selfishness, valuing above all the improvements of the mind – in short, truly human, and quite different from the lower animals. Once this contrast became familiar, people were constantly drawn to show that they belonged to the second, nobler, class (264–5).

But what were the lawgivers and other wise men themselves after? They were after power and the rewards of power: 'the first rudiments of morality, broached by skilful politicians, to render men useful to each other as well as tractable, were chiefly contrived that the ambitious might reap the more benefit from, and govern vast numbers of them with the greatest ease and security' (267).

Mandeville dismisses the counter-suggestion that morality owed anything in the first instance to religion: 'it was not any heathen religion or other idolatrous superstition, that first put man upon crossing his appetites and subduing his dearest inclinations, but the skilful management of wary politicians; and the nearer we search into human nature, the more we shall be convinced, that the moral virtues are the political offspring which flattery begot upon pride' (269).

As we shall see, Hume too is willing to give some of the credit to skilful politicians; but some only. Part of his argument is intended to show that what Mandeville describes cannot be the whole of the story. On this I think we shall in the end agree with Hume.

Francis Hutcheson was Hume's immediate predecessor in the moral sense school, and Hume certainly expected Hutcheson to welcome his work as a development of his own. But this expectation was not completely fulfilled: Hutcheson thought that the third book of the *Treatise* lacked 'a certain Warmth in the Cause of Virtue'.

Hutcheson starts by defining moral goodness as 'our idea of some quality apprehended in actions, which procures approbation, attended with desire of the agent's happiness', and moral evil as 'our idea of a contrary quality, which excites condemnation or dislike'. Approbation and condemnation, he suggests, are simple ideas, not further analysable. But when he says that moral goodness is 'our idea of some quality ...' he surely does not mean that moral goodness is literally an idea; he must mean rather that our idea of goodness is the idea of some quality that provokes approval in us. Yet, as we shall see, there is an important ambiguity hidden in this phrase.

Hutcheson's main concern is to distinguish moral goodness from natural goodness, which is just the power that anything has to produce pleasure, either directly or indirectly. He argues against any attempt to reduce moral to natural goodness – and hence to interpret moral judgments as indirect expressions of selfish motives – and, consequently, against any theory, such as that of Hobbes or that of the theological

24

moralists, which would make moral rightness or wrongness merely a matter of conformity or non-conformity to a law made by either a human or a divine superior and backed by sanctions in that superior's power to make us happy or miserable. He also rejects a more subtle reduction of morality to self-love, according to which we do indeed perceive some beauty in good actions that makes us love their agent, but which adds that our only motive for good actions is the desire to obtain the pleasure that we shall therefore find in reflecting on our own good actions.

Three propositions are central in Hutcheson's theory. (i) We have a motive of genuine benevolence; we desire the happiness of others as an end, not merely as a means (in any way) to our own happiness. (ii) We have a moral sense, a tendency immediately to approve of actions of certain kinds and to disapprove of others. (iii) The object of this moral sense is benevolence: we approve of actions because and in so far as we take these to express the motive of benevolence. Let us examine these in turn.

As for point (i), it is obvious that we ordinarily suppose there to be such a thing as benevolence. We respond differently to an action we take to have been done out of genuine goodwill towards ourselves, in contrast with one, equally beneficial to us, which we take to have been performed from the agent's calculated self-interest. Besides, it is most implausible to suppose that such apparent benevolence is always spurious. Parents really care for their children, and friends for their friends, we feel unfeigned compassion for the sufferings of others, and so on. To Mandeville's suggestion that cunning politicians have induced men, just by praise and flattery, by statues and panegyrics, to believe that there is public spirit, that it is excellent in itself, and moreover have led men to admire public spirit in others and to imitate it themselves, Hutcheson replies contemptuously: 'So easy a matter it seems to him, to quit judging of others by what we feel in ourselves! – for a person who is wholly selfish, to imagine others to be public-spirited. ... Yet this it seems statues and panegyrics can accomplish' (311).

Another rival suggestion is that we do indeed have benevolent feelings, but that 'we voluntarily bring this affection upon ourselves', believing that it will be in our interest to have it. To this Hutcheson replies that we cannot call up affections directly at will. This is true; yet we might be able to cultivate them over a period of time. Another suggestion is that we do desire the happiness of others, but only as a means to the pleasure that we shall experience through seeing them happy, or to avoid the pain we should feel in contemplating their misery. But if this was the true motive of compassion, we should satisfy it more easily by turning away from the sufferer than by trying to help him, and Hutcheson thinks we seldom do this. (But is he right?) Also, we want our family, our friends, and our country to be happy after we are dead, though we have no prospect of then being able to contemplate and enjoy their happiness (320, 323).

There are, as I have noted, some weaknesses in these arguments, but on the whole we can concede to Hutcheson, as to Shaftesbury, that there is such a thing as genuine benevolence. But it is a controversial question how large a part it can play both in human action and in moral thought. It is also disputable whether benevolence is a basic human instinct, or whether it is derived – as, we shall see, Hume suggests – from some more basic tendency to share feelings that we detect in others.

On point (ii), that we have a moral sense, Hutcheson explains that by a sense he means 'a determination of the mind, to receive any idea from the presence of an object which occurs to us, independent on our will'. A sense is, in effect, a capacity for having some sort of impression forced upon one immediately, without calculation or inference. It is undeniable that we have such an immediate differential response to voluntary actions, and that this is not just a matter of seeing those actions as beneficial or harmful to us, as sources or causes of pleasure or pain. For we respond differently to equally beneficial or equally harmful results if they come from voluntary actions on the one hand and from purely natural, physical, occurrences on the other, while we respond similarly to similarly benevolent actions, one of which benefits us whereas the other has no effect on us or is even harmful, and we condemn equally similarly bad actions even if one of them happens to benefit us. We can admire a gallant enemy, and dislike someone who, in a war, betrays his own country to our advantage. It is, as I said, undeniable that we have these immediate responses; the controversial question is whether they can somehow be explained away as derived from self-love. But Hutcheson argues that this cannot be done. If it is suggested that we approve of benevolent acts performed in the distant past because we imagine ourselves in the place of those who were benefited by them, why, he asks, do we not imagine ourselves in the place of those who were benefited by bad actions, and approve them accordingly? (310) He also argues that we could not be delighted by honour, or suffer from feelings of shame, unless we had a genuine, non-derivative, moral sense. Let us concede to Hutcheson that we have something like a moral sense;

26

but we shall have to come back to the question how it should be described and explained.

On point (iii), that the typical object of this moral sense is benevolence, Hutcheson argues that we do not morally approve even of what have been called the cardinal virtues on their own. Temperance would not be morally good if it showed no obedience to God, and made us no fitter for devotion, or the service of mankind, or the search after truth, than luxury. Courage, if it were mere contempt of danger, not connected with the defence of the innocent or the repairing of wrongs, or even with self-interest, would count as madness. Prudence, if it were used only for self-interest, would not be a virtue; and 'justice, or preserving a strict equality, if it has no regard to the good of mankind, the preservation of rights, and securing peace' is better fitted to characterize a pair of scales than a rational agent. These four are virtues only because and in so far as they are necessary to promote the public good and are associated with benevolent motives (315).

This third point, however, needs further consideration. First, if the object of moral approval is benevolence, what is the object of moral disapproval, which is a stronger and more basic component in moral thought? It will not do to say that we disapprove of actions in so far as they seem to us to express malevolence, because, as Hutcheson himself says, sheer uncomplicated malevolence is extremely rare. Even those whom we condemn usually have some moral justification for their behaviour. Robbers

> have their own sublime moral ideas of their party, as generous, courageous, trusty, nay honest too; and ... those we call honest and industrious, are imagined by them to be mean-spirited, selfish, churlish, or luxurious; on whom wealth is ill-bestowed which therefore they would apply to better uses, to maintain gallanter men, who have a right to a living as well as their neighbours, who are their professed enemies.

He adds that

> Perhaps never any men pursued vice long with peace of mind, without some such deluding imagination of moral good, while they may be still inadvertent to the barbarous and inhuman consequences of their actions ... the basest actions are dressed in some tolerable mask. What others call avarice, appears to the agent a prudent care of a family, or friends; fraud, artful conduct; malice and revenge, a just

sense of honour and a vindication of our right in possessions, of fame;
fire and sword, and desolation among enemies, a just thorough
defence of our country; persecution, a zeal for the truth, and for the
eternal happiness of men, which heretics oppose. In all these
instances, men generally act from a sense of virtue upon false
opinions, and mistaken benevolence; upon wrong or partial views of
public good, and the means to promote it; or upon very narrow
systems formed by like foolish opinions. It is not a delight in the
misery of others, or malice, which occasions the horrid crimes which
fill our histories; but generally an injudicious unreasonable
enthusiasm for some kind of limited virtue. (BM pp. 124–5).

These are tremendously important truths. What Hutcheson says here is
overwhelmingly confirmed by the horrid crimes which fill the histories
of the twentieth century. They too can be traced to a sense of virtue upon
false opinions, mistaken benevolence, unreasonable enthusiasm for
some kind of limited virtue, and misguided loyalty to narrow systems,
whether these are nations or parties or causes. But what are the
implications of this account for our question about the object of moral
disapproval? This cannot be simple malevolence, nor even simple lack of
benevolence. It must rather be neglect of the rights of others. But that
presupposes a moral system in which people have rights. Moral thinking
is more complicated and less direct than the initial statement of
Hutcheson's third point would suggest.

A closely related problem (which is the starting point of Hume's
theory of the artificial virtues) is that there are kinds of action, and
dispositions associated with them, of which we approve morally
although they do not express or incorporate benevolence. These include
respect for property rights, honesty, veracity, the keeping of agreements,
loyalty to one's king or country, and the various aspects of sexual
morality. And as we have just noted, we disapprove of the contrary
kinds of actions and dispositions even when they express or incorporate
benevolence, as they often do. We shall see in a moment how Hutcheson
deals with this problem about the content of morality. As an important
preliminary, he notes that 'benevolence' is a broad term: we must
distinguish at least three kinds of benevolence. One is a calm, extensive
goodwill directed equally towards all beings capable of happiness or
misery. Another is 'a calm deliberate affection ... toward the happiness
of certain smaller systems or individuals; such as patriotism ...
friendship, or parental affection' – but parental affection of a judicious,

self-controlled, sort. The third consists of various passions of love, pity,
sympathy, or what he calls 'congratulation', that is, immediate pleasure
in the observed happiness of someone else (331). But which, of these
three, is the true object of the moral sense? Hutcheson suggests that the
first, the reflective universal benevolence, is the best, while the second is
better than the third, though this, too, can be approved as long as it does
not conflict with either of the others. Even where it does so conflict it
offers some extenuation: we do not blame someone too much if he acts
either against the general happiness or against the long-term welfare of
some smaller group or individual that he cares for, if he does so from
immediate impulses of love, pity, or the like. All this is fair enough if
Hutcheson is just reporting on the direct responses of our moral sense,
but it would leave him without any determinate, systematic, morality.
He goes on, however, to offer a utilitarian account of the moral qualities
of actions as a guide to deciding what to do: 'the virtue is in a compound
ratio of the quantity of good, and number of enjoyers ... so that, that
action is best, which procures the greatest happiness for the greatest
numbers'. This seems to be the first occurrence in literature of this
famous formula. But, as Hutcheson uses it, it is not exposed to the charge
of indeterminacy. He says quite clearly that the key quantity is the
product of the degree of happiness and the number of people who have
that degree of happiness. It is a natural corollary that if different groups
derive different degrees of happiness from a proposed action, we should
sum all the resulting products, and hence that what should guide our
choice is simply the total quantity of happiness. He also insists that we
should take account of long-term and indirect results of actions, even
where these come about through choices of other agents, if these are in
some way provoked by the original action. This will explain some of the
complications in our moral thought which led Hume to speak of artificial
virtues. An action, Hutcheson says, may be wrong if, through the mistakes and corruption of others, it is likely to be made a precedent for evil
actions — that is, if, though good in itself, it will probably provoke men to
evil actions through some mistaken notion of their right. This, he says,

> is the reason that many laws prohibit actions in general, even when
> some particular instances of those actions would be very useful;
> because a universal allowance of them, considering the mistakes men
> would probably fall into, would be more pernicious than a universal
> prohibition; nor could there be any more special boundaries fixed
> between the right and wrong cases. (332–4)

It is, therefore, by a utilitarian method that Hutcheson explains those parts of the content of morality which do not fall immediately under the description of a moral sense approving of expressions of benevolence. Thus he derives rights from his moral sense. 'Whenever it appears to us, that a faculty of doing, demanding, or possessing any thing, universally allowed in certain circumstances, would in the whole tend to the general good, we say that any person in such circumstances, has a right to do, possess, or demand that thing.' On this ground he bases rights to self-defence, to the punishment of criminals, to the fruits of one's labour. To deprive people of the fruits of their labour 'takes away all motives to industry from self-love, or the nearer ties' – such as family affection – leaving no motive to industry except the weak one of general benevolence; 'nay, it exposes the industrious as a constant prey to the slothful, and sets self-love against industry'. Rights to commerce and rights based on contracts and promises have the same source, and so do other moral rules and attitudes. 'Marriage must be so constituted as to ascertain the offspring; otherwise we take away from the males one of the strongest motives to public good, *viz.* natural affection. ....' And the advantages of having 'unprejudiced arbitrators' and 'prudent directors' give men the right to 'constitute civil government, and to subject their alienable rights to the disposal of their governors, under such limitations as their prudence suggests'. These examples, he claims, show how our moral sense, 'by a little reflection upon the tendencies of actions, may adjust the rights of mankind' (353; BM pp. 160–6).

Nor, it seems, did Hutcheson shrink from the less palatable consequences of utilitarianism.

> If putting the aged to death, with all its consequences, really tends to
> the public good, and to the lesser misery of the aged, it is no doubt
> justifiable; nay, perhaps the aged choose it, in hopes of a future state.
> If a deformed, or weak race, could never, by ingenuity and art, make
> themselves useful to mankind, but should grow an absolutely
> unsupportable burden, so as to involve a whole state in misery, it is
> just to put them to death. (BM p. 122)

Admittedly these remarks occur in a passage where he is explaining that the 'absurd practices' which are found in some places are not evidence against a universal moral sense whose object is benevolence, that mistaken views are evidence of defective reasoning rather than of the lack of a moral sense. He is, none the less, committed to these hypothetical judgments.

Such derivations and conclusions, however, can still be disputed. Butler thought that we are not competent to perform these derivations for ourselves, but rather have to follow the unexplained directives of a conscience with which God has provided us, and which commands and approves of kinds of actions which are neither motivated by benevolence nor justifiable by us in terms of the general happiness, though we may suppose that God's aim in fitting us up with just such a conscience was to promote the general happiness. Hume also argues initially that the artificial virtues are not motivated by benevolence, though in the end he traces our approval of them to the indirect operation of sympathy, which interests us in the public good.

Whereas Hutcheson makes the total amount of good produced the test to be used in the choice of actions, he measures the virtue of agents (after the event) simply by the amount of benevolence their actions express. For example, if two agents each produce equal amounts of good, their virtue need not be equal, but will be inversely proportional to their abilities. Again, if an action is performed from mixed motives, partly benevolent and partly selfish, this reduces the virtue in so far as the action would not have been done if only the benevolent motive had been operating (BM pp. 110–14). What Hutcheson says here anticipates Kant's discussion of the moral worth of actions, and may have influenced it. But there is this vital difference (apart from the fact that Hutcheson is much clearer than Kant), that for Kant the uniquely valuable motive is not benevolence but a 'good will' which he equates (in man) with the sense of duty; benevolence, of any of Hutcheson's three kinds, would be put down merely as an inclination.[10]

Although Hutcheson has preferred the first, universal or utilitarian, sort of benevolence to the second, which aims, still in a reflective way, at the long-term good of a particular group or individual, he does give the latter an important role. 'There are nearer and stronger kinds of benevolence, when the objects stand in some nearer relations to ourselves, which have obtained distinct names; such as *natural affection*, *gratitude*, *esteem*.' Our having these stronger kinds of benevolence in closer relationships is a proof of 'the wise order in which human nature is formed for universal love, and mutual good offices' (341–2). Purely general benevolence, he argues, would be dissipated upon too many objects, and would therefore be inefficient; the tendency to show gratitude to benefactors, for example, concentrates benevolence and makes it more effective. Thus the greater strength of this second kind of benevolence is seen as a device for promoting the general happiness

31

which is the object of the first kind, but which the first kind, as a human motive, would often fail to promote effectively. This brings Hutcheson close to Butler's above-mentioned view. But he also notes that gratitude encourages benefactors by giving them an additional, self-interested, motive. Here, as in the remarks quoted earlier about industry and property, Hutcheson comes close to saying that some moral rules and dispositions are devices by which self-interest is harnessed so as to promote the general well-being; but he ascribes these devices not to men, as Hobbes and Mandeville had done, and as Hume was to do, but to God as the author of human nature; he thinks that gratitude, like parental affection, is natural and innate. Unlike Hume, he does not see this second kind of benevolence, 'confined generosity', as helping to cause the conflicts which another part of morality, Hume's artificial virtues, is needed to resolve.

But let us go back to Hutcheson's second main point, the thesis that we have a moral sense. As he says, we would not need a moral sense either to observe an agent's external action or to detect his motives. That a certain action was motivated by a genuine desire for the happiness of others is a matter of psychological fact, more or less decidable in quite ordinary ways. The special moral sense is needed to attach approval, and love for the agent, to an action already observed to be benevolent. But in calling this a sense, Hutcheson might have been using either of two different models, drawing attention to either of two rival analogies. Is moral sensing like what happens, according to Locke, in our perception of a primary quality like shape or number, where our sensations give us pretty correct information about something which is literally there in the objects? I see the table as square, and it is square, just as I see it. I see it as having four corners, and the set of its corners does indeed conform to my concept of four. Or is it more like what happens when I touch something very hot and feel pain? My pain sensation is a natural, immediate, non-inferential, non-willed response to something objective, but the pain that I feel does not inform me about anything like pain-as-I-feel-it in the object. Hutcheson makes it clear that he is using the second of these analogies, not the first. After distinguishing 'the idea of the external motion ... and its tendency to the happiness or misery of some sensitive nature' and the 'opinion of the affections in the agent', he says 'so far the idea of an action represents something external to the observer, really existing, whether he had perceived it or not, and having a real tendency to certain ends'; he must mean that it represents something external so far as it covers the two elements just distinguished. He contrasts with these

32

The perception of approbation or disapprobation arising in the observer, according as the affections of the agent are apprehended kind in their just degree, or deficient, or malicious. This approbation cannot be supposed an image of any thing external, more than the pleasures of harmony, of taste, of smell.

He admits that such a sense can fall into 'disorder', but he cannot see what the correcting of such a disorder could be 'except suggesting to its remembrance its former approbations, and representing the general sense of mankind' (371).

Hutcheson's original definition of moral goodness as 'our idea of some quality apprehended in actions, which procures approbation' might have been construed in either of two ways. On the first construal, we have the idea of some further quality in the action, additional to the benevolence but necessarily tied to it, a quality of approbation-demandingness. On the second, the quality which procures approbation is simply benevolence, but its being morally good consists in our seeing it in a certain way, namely as calling for benevolence and love: this is indeed 'our idea'.

If we followed the first construal, then we should be saying that the operation of the moral sense is like the perception of such a primary quality as squareness, except that now the objective quality we perceive is of a special prescriptive sort, being approbation-demandingness itself. Merely by perceiving it we are necessarily committed to the approbation in question. But if we followed the second construal, we should be saying that being morally good is – so far as its logical status is concerned – rather like being painful. It is simply being such as to provoke a certain subjective response, and that it provokes this response is entirely contingent upon the nature of the perceiver, though human beings are fairly uniform in this respect. Just as there might well be creatures who could touch red-hot iron without feeling pain, so there might well be creatures who could detect benevolence without feeling approbation. We just happen to be made as benevolence-approvers, much as we just happen to be made as heat-sensitive.

The doctrine of a moral sense is ambiguous between these interpretations, one of which makes the distinctively moral quality objective, the other of which makes it subjective. The remarks quoted show that Hutcheson opted firmly for the subjective interpretation, and so, as we shall see, did Hume. But when Butler was willing to call the faculty of drawing moral distinctions a moral sense, it must have been with the objective interpretation. When later thinkers spoke of moral intuitions rather than a moral sense, they wished to keep part of what Hutcheson meant – that this kind of response is immediate, non-inferential, non-willed, and nearly universal among men – but also to say something about which the 'moral sense' terminology is ambiguous, and which Hutcheson himself did not want to say, that the distinctively moral element, the approbation-demandingness, is objective and is necessarily attached to whatever may be the natural feature in which we find it – say, benevolence.

These distinctions lead to a problem. If we follow the subjective interpretation, we have to say that, from a reflective point of view, the moral force in favour of benevolence must be recognized as a contingent fact about ourselves. (Of course, this is compatible with its being a pretty powerful fact; after all, the way a piece of red-hot iron feels when I touch it is just a contingent fact about me – and most other human beings – but it is none the less a pretty powerful reason for me to take my hand away as quickly as I can.) But must we not admit, on reflection, that it does not *seem* to be so? We have some tendency to feel that the moral wrongness of a proposed act is an externally authoritative feature which tells us not to do this – which is part of what Clarke was getting at with his talk about necessary relations of fitness and unfitness. The objectivist interpretation of 'moral sense', the one that leads to the use of the term 'intuition' instead of 'sense', has an element of truth at least as a description of what *seems* to be going on when we respond to the morally relevant features of voluntary actions: moral approval and disapproval seem to reflect objective features in a way that the feeling of pain does not.

Hutcheson was criticized on these grounds by John Balguy. Hutcheson's view makes virtue depend on instincts, which might have been otherwise if the Creator had so decided. What, then, made God choose to implant in us these affections rather than others? If the answer is that God chose them because he is himself benevolent and approves of benevolence, then Balguy asks whether this disposition is a perfection in the deity. If we say it is, we are implicitly assuming that benevolence is intrinsically better than its contrary; we are postulating a morality whose validity does not depend on our instincts. Criticizing Hutcheson's original definition, Balguy says that merit (moral goodness) is a quality in actions which not only gains the approbation of the observer, but also *deserves* or is *worthy* of it. He appeals to Clarke's doctrine of the eternal and unalterable relations of things as a surer and nobler foundation for morality than 'the two instincts of *affection* and *moral sense*', saying that

Marginal notes: Butler & intuitionists; prob w/ subjective interp.; strength of objective interp.; Balguy vs Hume 'it is no more in the power of the Deity to make rational beings approve of ingratitude, perfidiousness, etc., than it is in his power to make them conclude, that a part of any thing is equal to the whole.' This may be an unfortunate example, since more recent mathematics tells us that this does occur with infinite sets (a proper sub-set may be correlated one-one with the set of which it is a sub-set); still, we can see what he means, and it is a natural objectivist reaction against the subjectivism of Hutcheson's theory (438–46).

Another problem concerns the preference which Hutcheson gives to the first kind of benevolence – the universally reflective or utilitarian kind – over the second – also reflective, but focused on smaller groups and individuals more closely related in some way to the agent – and to this second kind over the third – particular, ephemeral, impulses of love, pity, and the like. In what sense can one be better than another? If it is just a contingent fact that people do approve of each of these three kinds, but sometimes of one, sometimes of another, then that is all there is about it: there will be no question of one approval being more justified than another. However, there is no reason why approvals should not be the object of further approvals, no reason why Hutcheson himself should not approve of one kind of approval more than another. Moreover, if benevolence itself, and the moral sense that approves of it, can be seen as devices, as having some further point or function – either, as Hutcheson himself thought, by divine arrangement, or in some other way – then there could be a ground for his preference. It might well be that the universally reflective kind of benevolence is the one that mirrors most accurately this overall point or function, even if, as Hutcheson saw, the second kind may, as a human motive, often be a more effective means to this end, and this may sometimes be true also of the third kind.

Clear and well-argued though it is, Hutcheson's theory leaves us still with two problems. One concerns the explanation of the content of morality. Can this content be adequately explained in terms of innate and universal benevolent dispositions (of the three kinds) and a tendency to approve of benevolence, combined with various true and false beliefs? The other concerns the status of morality. Are moral judgments and beliefs correctly described as the products of a moral sense, construed in what I have distinguished as the subjectivist way, or must we accommodate somehow the claim that there are qualities in actions which not only gain but also deserve approbation and disapprobation?

Joseph Butler, Bishop of Durham, stands in an interesting way between the rationalist and moral sense schools. He distinguishes two possible

> ways in which the subject of morals may be treated. One begins from inquiring into the abstract relations of things: the other from a matter of fact, namely, what the particular nature of man is … from whence it proceeds to determine what course of life it is, which is correspondent to this whole nature. In the former method the conclusion is expressed thus, that vice is contrary to the nature and reason of things: in the latter, that it is a violation or breaking in upon our own nature.

The first of these methods is plainly Clarke's, and Butler does not reject it; on the contrary, he gives it a general endorsement: 'The first seems the most direct formal proof, and in some respects the least liable to cavil and dispute.' But he does not himself pursue it: 'The following discourses proceed chiefly in this latter method', which, he says, 'is in a peculiar manner adapted to satisfy a fair mind, and is more easily applicable to the several particular relations and circumstances in life'. We may find, however, that the way in which Butler bases morality on human nature involves, after all, an implicit use of Clarke's method (375).

Butler's primary purpose is to argue that the injunction 'Follow nature', or 'Act in accordance with human nature', is not to be interpreted as meaning or entailing 'Do whatever at any moment you feel most inclined to do.' He argues that human nature is not a mere collection or sequence of impulses, but a system, which he compares with a watch. Just as, when you see how the parts of a watch fit together, you can tell that it is adapted to measure time, so when you see how the parts of human nature fit together, you can tell that it is 'adapted to virtue'.

In this system of human nature he distinguishes four parts. There are various particular passions, that is, desires for various particular objects and feelings associated with such desires. There is benevolence, the desire that others should be happy. There is self-love, a reflective passion which aims at the happiness of the individual who has it, that is, at the satisfaction as far as possible of all his desires, future ones as well as present ones. And there is another reflective element, conscience, which approves or disapproves of one's own actions – but not only actions. The mind can take a view of what passes within itself, its propensions, aversions, passions, affections … and of the several actions consequent

36

thereupon.' Butler's conscience corresponds roughly to Hutcheson's moral sense, but he thinks of it as being focused inwards rather than outwards: it is of our own feelings, motives, and actions that conscience primarily approves or disapproves (390).

Butler has little difficulty in showing that there are these four parts of human nature – arguing against Hobbes, for example, that there is a natural principle of benevolence in man, which cannot be explained away as mere love of power. He concedes that love of power may often be mixed up with benevolence, but if there were nothing but the love of power at work, would it not express itself more easily and directly in cruelty? Like Shaftesbury, and against Hobbes, Butler concludes that a full survey of these parts of human nature shows that 'it is as manifest, that *we were made for society, and to promote the happiness of it*; *as that we were intended to take care of our own life, and health, and private good*' (388–91).

To the objection that men also have tendencies which lead them to harm one another Butler says that this shows only that the system can get out of order – and it can equally get out of order in such a way that the individual agent harms himself. In either case the source of the trouble is 'ungoverned passions': particular passions, though in themselves harmless and indeed beneficial and necessary elements in human nature, may become too strong and express themselves in ways that are not suitably controlled by the two reflective elements, self-love and conscience. But suppose that someone's passions are disordered in this way; will he not be following *his* nature if he obeys them, going against self-love and conscience? Again, suppose that some immoral course of action, of which his conscience disapproves, will bring him greater happiness, even in the long term, than acting morally would, and suppose that his self-love happens to be stronger than his conscience; will this man not be following *his* nature if he obeys self-love and acts immorally? Butler says no. He appeals to the natural superiority of self-love over the particular passions, and to the natural supremacy or authority of conscience over all the other elements.

But just what is this superiority or authority? Butler has several answers. First, there is the suggestion that, as with the watch, we can see how the system of human nature is meant to fit together and work as a whole; though disordered conditions occur, we can tell what its healthy or flourishing state would be. He does not, I think, mean that the watch has a function merely in so far as its maker or its user intends it to do something, namely to tell the time, and that man also has a function in that his maker, God, intends him to behave in a certain way. He thinks rather that the function of the watch or of man is intrinsic, not purely derivative from a maker's purpose. There is something that is the healthy or flourishing condition of each in itself. Secondly, Butler thinks it is obvious that self-love is superior to the particular passions, that everyone will agree that a man who, foreseeing the danger of certain ruin, still rushed into it for the sake of a present gratification would be acting against his true nature; if this is granted, he can use it as an analogy to explain and support the natural supremacy of conscience. Thirdly, he speaks of conscience 'from its very nature manifestly claiming superiority over all others: insomuch that you cannot form a notion of this faculty, conscience, without taking in judgement, direction, superintendency.' However, this third point shows only that conscience embodies a *claim* to authority, not that it *has* authority, that in understanding what it is we must endorse that claim. His second argument shows that it would be in a manner arbitrary, though not incoherent, to allow the superiority of self-love to the particular passions but to deny the supremacy of conscience; but a sufficiently tough-minded opponent might deny both. The greatest weight falls upon the first argument. We can perhaps understand the healthy or flourishing condition of some complex system in either of two related ways: it may be the state in which it is to some extent self-maintaining and self-perpetuating, or, again, it may be that which gives some point to all (or nearly all) parts of the system, allowing each to contribute somehow to the others. What Butler is claiming, then, is that the healthy state of man as an active, purposive, choosing being is that in which conscience is supreme.

We could challenge this doctrine in several ways. It conceals an important indeterminacy. In general someone's personality will be more integrated, more harmonious, if his choices of action are such as his own moral thinking can approve; but this may yield no precise moral conclusions, since different people's consciences can approve of different things. Also, conscience can be a disruptive rather than an integrating force: some people have had the bad luck to develop forms of conscience with which other ineradicable parts of their character cannot be reconciled. A change in the demands of conscience may be the only way of increasing harmony. But suppose that we set all such difficulties aside, and concentrate on cases where the dominant position of a conscience which prescribes what is widely recognized as morality does achieve a fairly integrated personality; we may still ask what is the *force* of

Butler's thesis that virtue is (then) in accord with human nature. It may be in part a hypothetical imperative: if these (perhaps fortunate) people prefer to have integrated personalities, as they probably will, then they should act morally so as to maintain this condition. Secondly, we have here an *argumentum ad homines* addressed to those who have used the slogan 'Follow nature' as a justification for some immoral pattern of behaviour. They have made the mistake of trying to argue from an 'is' to an 'ought', or at least to a 'not ought not': 'Since my nature demands this, it cannot be that I ought not to do it'. Butler is turning the tables on those who argue thus, showing that *if* one could derive moral conclusions from psychological facts, conclusions very different from theirs would (often) follow. But, thirdly, I think Butler does want to derive an objective categorical imperative here, to say that the ought-judgments of the morality in question are authoritatively validated by the fact that they issue from a conscience whose supremacy goes with a flourishing state of the human agent. But if this is to be anything more than the above-mentioned hypothetical imperative, the implicit argument will require a categorically imperative premiss, say (in Clarke's terms) that it is *fitting* that the agent should flourish and should so act as to maintain his own flourishing state. And this will be a basic, not rationally supported, value judgment: in short an 'intuition' of an alleged prescriptive truth. Much of the plausibility of Butler's case is due to the fact that these different suggestions are not distinguished but run together.

There are several other important themes in Butler's work. One is the sharp distinction he draws between self-love and the particular passions. Hobbes's view that men are entirely selfish lumps these two together, arguing, in effect, that because some passion or desire is in the agent, is part of his make-up, it is therefore selfish. Of course, Butler concedes, an agent can be motivated only by motives that he has; but this does not show that every agent is selfish in any interesting or important sense which marks off one possible sort of conduct from another. What is usefully marked off by the term 'selfishness' or 'self-love' is simply the desire for one's own general, long-term, happiness; this is quite different from a desire for food or drink or revenge. Not only are they distinct, so that there can be motives located in the agent which are not selfish; there must be these particular passions, or self-love would have nothing to do. You cannot aim at happiness unless there are things that will give you the pleasures and satisfactions that make up happiness, and these must be the objects of other, particular, desires. The operation of self-love involves the operation of particular passions, so that self-love just could not have been the whole of human nature. Hence follows also the 'paradox of hedonism', that in general you cannot get happiness by aiming directly at it: you must develop other aims or interests as well; so 'even from self-love we should endeavour to get over all inordinate regard to, and consideration of ourselves' (415–17).

There is, as Butler admits, one exception to this argument; even if there were no particular passions, self-love could still aim at and perhaps achieve the removal and avoidance of pain. Pain does not arise only from the frustration of desires, so its elimination could be pursued directly, without any other desires being involved. But this is only a small exception; clearly when most people speak of happiness they mean something much more positive than the avoidance of pain. The particular passions, then, though distinct from self-love, are not in general contrary to it: it needs them in order to function.

This distinction enables Butler to point out that the particular passions usually have external objects, and hence that benevolence, though it too has an external object, the happiness of others, can still be related to self-love just as any particular passion is. The happiness of someone else is something which I can desire just as I may desire food or drink or revenge, and if I succeed in bringing it about I shall get satisfaction from doing so: the fulfilment of this desire can contribute to my own happiness just as much as the fulfilment of any other desire. Though benevolence is distinct from self-love, it is no more contrary to it than is any particular passion. It might be objected that though as motives these two are not opposed, yet in practice the actions required for their pursuit are often contrary, that one can usually make others happy only by sacrificing things that would contribute more to one's own happiness. But Butler, rather optimistically, denies this, sticking to the claim that you can get happiness from the successful pursuit of benevolence as well as from the successful pursuit of any other desire, and that in the case of failure 'the benevolent man has clearly the advantage; since endeavouring to do good considered as a virtuous pursuit, is gratified by its own consciousness, i.e., is in a degree its own reward' (419–20).

Though Butler has thus made some sound points against Hobbes, he has not damaged Hobbes's central argument. This could be restated, after all the necessary concessions have been made to Butler's criticisms, by saying that the collection of particular passions and self-love and limited benevolence (directed towards family, friends, benefactors, and so on) that men naturally have is likely to generate extreme conflicts, if

40

not between individuals, still between small mutually hostile groups; if men in civil society have conscientious feelings which restrain or resolve these conflicts, it still needs to be explained where these come from and how they are sustained.

Butler, however, takes an optimistic view – surely far too optimistic – that benevolence and self-love, if sufficiently calm and reflective, will almost always prescribe the same actions, and that the commands of conscience will also coincide with both of these. 'Self-love then, though confined to the interest of the present world, does in general perfectly coincide with virtue; and leads us to one and the same course of life.' But if they do not quite coincide in this world, we can rely on God and the next world to make the coincidence perfect. 'Duty and interest are perfectly coincident; for the most part in this world, but entirely and in every instance if we take in the future and the whole; this being implied in the notion of a good and perfect administration of things' (408–9).

Butler insists that there is nothing wrong with self-love. 'Self-love in its due degree is as just and morally good, as any affection whatever. ... Neither does there appear any reason to wish self-love were weaker in the generality of the world, than it is.' If people had more self-love, they would avoid the follies and vices that particular passions produce when they go to excess (384–5). There is even a curious passage in which Butler seems to give self-love the last word.

> It may be allowed, without any prejudice to the cause of virtue and religion, that our ideas of happiness and misery are of all our ideas the nearest and most important to us; that they will, nay, if you please, that they ought to prevail over those of order, and beauty, and harmony, and proportion, if there should ever be, as it is impossible there ever should be, any inconsistence between them: though these last too, as expressing the fitness of actions, are real as truth itself.

He seems to be subordinating both Clarke's principles and Wollaston's to self-love.

> Let it be allowed, though virtue or moral rectitude does indeed consist in affection to and pursuit of what is right and good, as such; yet that when we sit down in a cool hour, we can neither justify to ourselves this or any other pursuit, till we are convinced that it will be for our happiness, or at least not contrary to it. (423)

Butler takes care to identify the benevolence of which he speaks with a reflective principle that considers 'distant consequences, as well as the immediate tendency of an action'. But it is Hutcheson's second kind of benevolence that he means, not the first, universalistic or utilitarian, kind: 'the care of some persons, suppose children and families, is particularly committed to our charge by nature and Providence; ... there are other circumstances, suppose friendship or former obligations, which require that we do good to some, preferably to others.' If, of two equally well-qualified candidates for a post, one is our friend, it is quite in order, even obligatory, to exert ourselves on his behalf (434).

But even when he has thus identified benevolence, Butler still insists that it is not the whole of virtue: 'as we are not competent judges, what is upon the whole for the good of the world; there may be other immediate ends appointed us to pursue, besides that one of doing good, or producing happiness'. Treachery, indecency, meanness are to be, and are, disapproved; greatness of mind, fidelity, honour, strict justice are to be approved without reference to their tendency to produce happiness. God's goodness, perhaps, is pure benevolence; but ours is not and cannot be. 'Since this is our constitution; falsehood, violence, injustice, must be vice in us, and benevolence to some preferably to others, virtue, abstracted from all consideration of the overbalance of evil or good, which they may appear likely to produce.' He explicitly argues against Hutcheson here. 'The happiness of the world is the concern of him, who is the Lord and Proprietor of it: nor do we know what we are about, when we endeavour to promote the good of mankind in any ways, but those which he has directed;' but he adds, 'that is indeed in all ways, not contrary to veracity and justice' (427n, 434–5).

He is saying that the general happiness is, indeed, from God's point of view, the ultimate object of the moral exercise. But we are not competent to aim explicitly and directly at it; we have to follow the directives of the conscience with which God has provided us, and it prescribes various other virtues as well as benevolence, and even where it does prescribe benevolence, it is the particular rather than the universal kind. Since we have good reason to doubt our own practical wisdom, this view would be acceptable if we could be as confident as Butler is about the divine origin of our actual consciences. But if we either deny or doubt the existence of a god, or suspect that our specific conscientious responses may have developed in some other way, we may well think it appropriate to look more closely at those elements in conventional morality which we cannot easily derive from, or even reconcile with, the promoting of the general happiness – that is, roughly, what Hume calls the artificial virtues. Some of these may need to be revised; but it may turn out that some of them can be defended on other grounds as restrictions on the ways in which we can 'endeavour to promote the good of mankind'.

There is, finally, a remark of Butler's which reveals how he stands between the rationalist and moral sense schools. He speaks of 'a moral faculty; whether called conscience, moral reason, moral sense, or divine reason; whether considered as a sentiment of the understanding, or as a perception of the heart, or, which seems the truth, as including both' (429).

This appears to be an echo from Aristotle's *Nicomachean Ethics* (1139b4–5), where rational choice is said to be either desiring intellect or intellectual desire. It stresses not only the intellectual and the emotional sides of the moral faculty, but also an inextricable connection between them. Price changes this to 'a perception of the understanding and a feeling of the heart' (688); but Butler surely intends the subtler, paradoxical, interconnection. I entirely agree that this is how moral experience presents itself to us: Butler is right about the moral phenomenology. But it remains paradoxical, and we may well want to look beyond the experience itself for some further explanation of it.

When we turn back to Hume, after this survey of the views of some of his predecessors, we shall find that the same themes recur, that he takes up these earlier disputes but also carries them several steps further.

III

HUME'S PSYCHOLOGY OF ACTION

(*TREATISE* II iii 3)

It has been usual, Hume says, to speak of the combat between passion and reason, and to say that virtue consists in conformity to reason, indeed, in the victory of reason over the passions. But, he maintains, this whole way of thinking is in error : first, reason can never be a motive to any action of the will, and, secondly, it can never oppose passion in the direction of the will. Reason and passion cannot conflict with one another, so reason can never conquer passion.

Here, as elsewhere, Hume divides the work of the understanding into 'demonstration' and 'probability'; the first concerns 'relations of ideas', which yield, in particular, mathematical knowledge, the second all empirical and causal knowledge or belief. He thinks it is obvious that demonstrative knowledge or reasoning alone is never a cause of any action. It influences action only in so far as it helps us to work out causes and effects, which it can do only in association with the second sort of work of the understanding, probability.

If we expect pleasure or pain from any object, we are thereby attracted or repelled, and so motivated to action. Anything that we see to be connected as a cause with the original object as its effect will also attract or repel us in the same way. So causal knowledge or belief does indeed influence action. But, Hume says, the impulse here does not arise from reason, but is only directed by it. The attraction or repulsion comes originally from the expectation of pleasure or pain. It could never matter to us, with a view to action, that A causes B, if both A and B were indifferent to us. So reason alone, even including 'probability', can never produce any action.

Hume goes on to argue that since reason alone cannot produce action,

44

it is equally unable to prevent it; it cannot by itself oppose any volition. It could oppose one volition only by setting up a contrary one, and this, we have seen, it cannot do. So there can be no literal conflict between reason and passion: 'Reason is, and ought only to be the slave of the passions, and can never pretend to any other office than to serve and obey them.' (Here 'ought only to be' must mean merely that it is not the case that reason ought not to be the slave of the passions; Hume is denying a moral proposition rather than asserting one.)

He supports this conclusion with a further argument. He contrasts a passion, which is 'an original existence', with ideas, beliefs, and so on which have a representative function. Since truth and reason concern the agreement between such items and whatever they represent, only some rival representation could be contrary to them; but a passion is not a representation.

Hume allows, indeed, that a passion may be contrary to reason in so far as it is accompanied by some judgment or opinion, and this can happen in either of two ways. First, a passion such as hope or fear or grief or joy or despair or security may be founded on the supposition of the existence of certain objects, and reason may point out that these do not in fact exist. Hume means that the fear of ghosts, for example, is contrary to reason, since there aren't any ghosts, or that my joy at the prospect of winning the lottery is contrary to reason if I have no good grounds for expecting to win. Secondly, a passion may be said to be contrary to reason when in some action to which it leads we choose means insufficient for the intended result, and make mistakes about the relevant relations of cause and effect. For example, he would presumably say that it is contrary to reason to try to cut down an oak tree with a table knife, or to try to make a perpetual motion machine, and the passions expressed in such attempts can be called, by association, contrary to reason. But even in these cases it is, strictly speaking, not the passion that is contrary to reason but the belief which precedes or accompanies it. We could add that where some purpose is correspondingly based on a true belief or a correct calculation it may be said to be in accordance with reason or reasonable or rational, but again it is, strictly speaking, not the passion that is in accordance with reason, but the associated or presupposed belief.

Hume throws in here two memorable examples. ''Tis not contrary to reason to prefer the destruction of the whole world to the scratching of my finger. 'Tis not contrary to reason for me to chuse my total ruin, to prevent the least uneasiness of an *Indian* or person wholly unknown to me.' And he adds, ' 'Tis as little contrary to reason to prefer even my own acknowledg'd lesser good to my greater, and have a more ardent affection for the former than the latter.' But these remarks involve several different principles. His previous argument assumed that the motive for any will or action was an unexpected pleasure or pain, and that reason could influence choice by pointing out causes of pleasure or pain. But now he is saying that desires (which are presumably the ultimate motives for choice and action) need not depend on expected pleasures or pain. Presumably the destruction of the whole world would cause me — ignoring everyone else — more pain, or a greater loss of possible pleasure, than the scratching of my finger. If the Indian, or whoever it is, is wholly unknown to me, I shall presumably get no pleasure, and avoid no distress, by saving him from uneasiness (except in so far as this will gratify this unexplained whim), whereas my total ruin will be unpleasant in the extreme. Hume says explicitly that I can prefer what I know to be a lesser good to a greater. The greatness of the goods cannot then be measured by the degree of my preference, but perhaps by the amount of pleasure they will bring. This extension of his thesis is paradoxical, yet consistency requires it. Since a desire is an original existence, logically distinct from the expectation of pleasure from the desired object (which, being a belief, has a representative function), it must be logically possible for desires to fail to be correlated with expected pleasures, and then reason cannot require that they should be so correlated. The tough-mindedness which Hume shows here also serves to counter arguments of the sort we have found Butler using (page 38 above). If it were conceded that reason forbids one to prefer a lesser good, we should be granting the rational superiority of self-love or prudence to particular passions, and then it might seem arbitrary to draw the line and refuse to recognize an analogous supremacy of conscience.

This completes Hume's positive case. But he also tries to explain how the mistake which he is correcting has arisen. There is a distinction between 'violent passions' and 'calm desires and tendencies, which, tho' they be real passions, produce little emotion in the mind, and are more known by their effects than by the immediate feeling or sensation'. What is, according to Hume, properly called reason is often associated with these calm passions in opposition to more violent ones, and then we either do not notice that the calm passion is at work, or confuse it with the reasoning and beliefs with which it is associated and which it resembles at least in being different from a violent passion, in not stirring

46

up the mind, and so suppose that it is reason alone that is opposing the violent passions.

Harrison sums it up well: what Hume is getting at is that beliefs move us to action only if they are relevant to the satisfaction of a passion, and that reasoning, whether demonstrative or probable, affects our actions only in so far as it produces beliefs which are so relevant.[1] But it is to be noted that in order to defend this claim Hume has to postulate the presence of calm passions in some cases where we are initially inclined to say that reason is doing the work.

What should we say about this psychological theory? A possible objection – which was, indeed, made later by Reid – is that Hume is changing the meaning of the term 'reason' to suit his purpose, and that we do commonly use it, and related words like 'reasonable', to distinguish a concern for one's overall or long-term happiness from the pursuit of an immediate desire to the neglect of all other considerations. There may also be a use of these words such that reason will be said to involve or require some respect for the interests of other people. However, Hume is not making a merely verbal point, and we need not quarrel over the use of words. He has, after all, admitted that the operations of the calm passions are often called reason, and even if he were to concede that this is a conventional and allowable use of the word, he could and would insist that what is thus called reason is, in its true nature, very different from either mathematical knowledge and calculation or empirical and causal knowledge or belief, or any combination of these; he would argue that for an adequate psychological understanding of what is going on we have to see that these other kinds of 'reason' involve a *concern* for one's future well-being, or a *concern* for other people, which is analogous to the things that we explicitly recognize as passions or desires, even though this concern is sometimes an inferred, rather than a directly observed or introspected, mental element.

To this extent Hume's view is well-argued and defensible. Yet, in the light of our survey of earlier eighteenth-century moralists, we must say that he has not dealt adequately with his real opponents; he has not explicitly formulated or criticized the views to which his own is opposed. Someone like Clarke, for example, might well concede that Hume's model of choice, will, and action is correct for all ordinary cases *where moral considerations do not play any significant part*, but say that where such considerations do come in, we have something radically different from what his model allows. A relation of fitness, Clarke might say, is out there in the objects. It is a hard fact, indeed a necessary one, that a certain sort of action is fitting in relation to a certain situation. My judgment about this fitness has, therefore, in Hume's terms, a representative quality. Yet this judgment, my awareness of this fitness, is also in itself a motive to action. Like a passion, it has some motivating force, and yet it is not a purely 'original existence', such as Hume takes all passions to be. It is, Butler says, both a sentiment of the understanding and a perception of the heart. It has inextricably interwoven in it the representative character and the motivating character which Hume thinks can belong only to distinct items. And, Clarke or Butler might add, this mental element can have these two interwoven aspects just because the fitness of which it is a perception is something intrinsically and objectively prescriptive: the situation necessarily *demands* the action which fits it.

The opposing case here is strengthened by the consideration that Hume's own analysis, as we noted, is in part a psychological theory, dealing in inferred entities rather than ones of which the agent is immediately conscious. When someone goes against a present desire in the interest of his own long-term happiness, Hume has to say that what is at work here is a *concern* for future happiness, something that has the psychological status of a desire, though the agent may not self-consciously feel it as a desire. Similarly, when someone acts in what he regards as a morally obligatory way at the expense even of his long-term interest, Hume has to say that sentiments are somehow at work; but this may not be obvious to the agent. If Clarke, on the other hand, says that what is at work is not anything that has the status of a desire, but a rational perception that it is fitting that a being who preserves his identity through time and can foresee his future states should respond to possible happiness or misery in the future – the remoter future as well as the immediate future – he is not flying in the face of clearly observed psychological facts, but is putting forward a rival theory. And, for what this is worth, it is a theory that has some basis in our ordinary ways of speaking, one that reflects, though it also develops and makes more explicit, notions that we ordinarily have about our own behaviour. And the same is true about a case where someone sacrifices both immediate desires and long-term interest to the welfare of others or to some principle of honesty or fidelity or justice. Hume will say that there is a passion of some sort at work here, though it is not recognized and does not present itself as such. Clarke will say that what does the work is the perception of a fitness which in itself necessarily requires the action in question. These are two rival theories; each is committed in its own way to certain inferred or postulated entities. We have no overwhelming or immediately cogent reason for adopting one theory and rejecting the other, but will have to decide in the end which gives the best overall explanation of the whole range of relevant data and experiences.

I suggest, then, that we cannot take Hume to have established his view about 'the influencing motives of the will'; but neither can we reject his view. This issue must remain unsettled until we see how the rest of his theory develops and supports this psychological thesis.

There is, indeed, another way in which reason can be opposed by passion, which Hume fails to notice. Suppose that I have one of his calm passions, say a concern for my own future health, and also have a well-founded belief about the means to this, say that drinking large quantities of alcohol is likely to damage my health in the long run. Together these will provide me with a motive for not drinking large quantities of alcohol. But suppose that I also have a strong present desire to do just this, either because I like the immediate sensations of drinking wine, beer, whisky, and so on, or because I enjoy the social atmosphere of conviviality that goes with drinking, or perhaps because I am already addicted to alcohol and simply feel that I must drink. Then there is a conflict between this motive and the one generated by the calm passion, my concern for my future health. So far all this is in accord with Hume's theory. But then what may happen is that, by a psychological trick of unconscious rationalization, I may reject or put out of my mind the well-founded belief that drinking large quantities of alcohol is likely to damage my health. Whereas we previously had calm passion united with well-founded belief in opposition to present desire, we now have an unholy alliance of calm passion with present desire opposing and perhaps suppressing well-founded belief. This sort of thing certainly can happen – in fact it happens all the time. Indeed, it should be obvious that if, as Hume agrees, one passion together with reason can oppose another passion, then the two passions together can oppose reason, since the only way in which they can flourish happily together is by dismissing the inconvenient belief which brings them into conflict with one another.

But though this is a phenomenon which Hume does not notice, and which literally falsifies his thesis that reason alone cannot be opposed to passion, it is not really at variance with his essential line of thought. It does not prove that reason can oppose any single passion on its own, nor that it can by itself initiate any course of action, let alone that it can

49

govern and direct a whole course of life. All it proves is that reason can oppose and be opposed by some combination of passions. Reason may show that two passions cannot flourish together, that one or other of them must go unfulfilled, and in consequence the conjunction of these passions may brush reason aside, suppressing this unwanted information.

IV

MORALITY NOT BASED ON REASON

(*TREATISE* III i 1)

In the first two sections of Book III of the *Treatise* Hume argues that moral distinctions are not derived from reason and that they are derived from a moral sense. This looks straightforward, and seems to show merely that he is agreeing with Shaftesbury and Hutcheson against Clarke and Wollaston and Balguy. But in fact what he says is riddled with ambiguities: it is not clear for what meaning of 'reason' he is saying that morality is not based on reason, and it is not clear exactly how we are to interpret 'moral sense' or to understand how moral distinctions are due to it.

In saying that moral distinctions are not derived from reason, does Hume mean only that they are not reached by demonstrative reasoning analogous to that which establishes mathematical conclusions? Or is he saying something stronger than this, that they are not derivable from any true beliefs, and hence are not objects of knowledge? Or something still stronger, that drawing moral distinctions is not a matter of having beliefs at all? The first of these would be compatible with several different positive views, including what I called, when commenting on Hutcheson, the objectivist interpretation of 'moral sense': according to this interpretation, moral sense is analogous to the perception of a primary quality, it is a faculty which discerns moral differences which are literally there to be perceived. But this view would be ruled out by the second or the third meaning of the thesis that moral distinctions are not derived from reason. The second would allow moral sense to be analogous to the perception of a secondary quality, where, for example, we ordinarily *believe* that something is, quite literally, red as we see red, but in itself it is not so; thus this second meaning might go with an *error*

51

we call it *Light at it*
may not be
what
interp # 3
allows

theory of moral judgments.[1] The third meaning would make moral sense, if it was admitted at all, analogous to the perception of pain, and would go with an explicitly non-descriptive (emotive or prescriptive) analysis of moral judgments.[2]

There are remarks in Hume's text which point in these different directions. Thus he starts by referring to his distinction (drawn first in Book I) between impressions and ideas, and suggests that the problem is '*Whether 'tis by means of our* ideas *or* impressions *we distinguish betwixt vice and virtue, and pronounce an action blameable or praiseworthy?*' This makes it look as if the view against which he is arguing is merely that moral distinctions depend on relations between ideas, that is, demonstrative reasoning, leaving it open that they might depend upon correct impressions and possess empirical truth. The same suggestion is given by the next few remarks, which give, as the account which he is rejecting, a précis of Clarke's doctrine of eternal fitnesses.

But (as we shall see) he says something quite different at the end of this section, and in any case his main argument offers a contrary indication. This uses as one premiss the conclusion of the section discussed in chapter III, that reason alone can have no influence on action. Combining this with the second premiss, that morality is practical, that it does produce or prevent actions, Hume concludes that morality cannot be derived from reason alone. Now if the conclusion here were intended merely to rule out a demonstrative derivation of morality, the first premiss would need to say only that demonstrative knowledge or reasoning alone cannot influence action. But the argument of II iii 3 explicitly makes a stronger claim than this, that neither demonstration nor probability nor any combination of them can, by itself, support or oppose an action. The conclusion of II iii 3, conjoined with the second premiss that morality is (by itself) practical, would entail that morality cannot be derived from any combination of reasoning, knowledge, and belief alone, whether *a priori* or empirical, and whether the beliefs are true or false. We may surmise that Hume himself was not quite clear about what he was doing; perhaps he set out only to argue against rationalists like Clarke and Wollaston, but found that he had, without intending this, developed arguments with more sweeping implications. It may, therefore, be impossible to find *the correct* interpretation of what Hume says; but we can examine and evaluate some of the different arguments which can be constructed with his materials.

Hume's second premiss, that morality is practical, that 'morals … have an influence on the actions and affections', must, if we are to get a valid argument, be read as meaning or entailing something like this: the state of mind which is the making of moral judgments and moral distinctions has, by itself, and just because it is that state, an influence on actions. If we conjoin this with the strong premiss which Hume thinks he has established as the conclusion of II iii 3, that knowledge, beliefs, and reasoning (of any kinds) alone do not influence actions, we can validly draw the conclusion that the state of mind in question does not consist wholly of knowledge, beliefs, and reasoning of any kinds.

However, as we found in chapter III, Hume has not really established the conclusion which would be the major premiss of this argument, since he has not examined and disposed of Clarke's rival theory, though he has correctly pointed out that Clarke has not actually produced any demonstration of his alleged necessary truths. There is no conclusive argument yet on either side. In fact the position is even worse for Hume than this would suggest, if the premiss he wants is that knowledge, beliefs, and reasoning (of any kind) alone do not influence actions. To undermine this, it is not necessary that anything like Clarke's view should be true; it is enough that someone should believe it to be true. For if Clarke, say, believes that there is a necessary fitness which requires him, in circumstances of kind X, to do Y, and also believes that the present circumstances are of kind X, will not these two beliefs together give Clarke a motive for doing Y? Even if Clarke's moral theory is false, the mere fact that he sincerely holds it is sufficient to falsify the strong premiss which Hume seems to be using here. It is evident that there can be sets of moral and factual beliefs which are, by themselves, motives to action.

There is, on the other hand, a weaker premiss which is much more defensible, and which emerges more clearly as a conclusion from the arguments of II iii 3. This is that nothing made up of demonstrative reasoning, causal knowledge, and factual information of ordinary sorts can by itself influence action, without the help of some passion or desire. The complete failure of Clarke and his followers to produce the demonstrations of which they speak, and the weakness of the analogy on which Clarke relies between mathematical fitting and moral fitness, makes this premiss highly plausible. But if we conjoin it with the one which says that the state of mind which is the making of moral distinctions does by itself influence actions, the conclusion we draw is that that state of mind cannot be made up merely of demonstrative reasoning, causal knowledge, and ordinary factual information. This would be a result of some importance, since it would rule out all

53

varieties of naturalism. But it would leave open the possibility of a non-natural objectivism, an intuitionism such as was explicitly adopted by Hume's successors, Price and Reid, and more recently by Moore, Prichard, and Ross. There might be some non-ordinary sort of what was still factual information, some special sort of belief or even knowledge supplied by a moral sense as the objectivist interpretation understands it, which does make moral distinctions that can in and by themselves influence action. Consequently, though this conclusion would fulfil one interpretation of Hume's programme of showing that such distinctions are derived from a moral sense and not from reason, it would be a more modest conclusion than the one which emerged from Hume's argument on the previous reading.

But, whichever of these two interpretations of Hume's major premiss we follow, there is, as Harrison points out, another way in which his conclusion can be evaded.[3] We could simply deny the minor premiss, that the state of mind which is the making of moral judgments and distinctions has, *by itself*, an influence on actions. We could say that just seeing that this is right and that is wrong will not tend to make someone do this or refrain from that: he must also *want* to do whatever is right. That is, we could deny the *intrinsic* action-guidingness of moral judgments. This would, of course, draw the teeth of Hume's argument. Whatever conclusion we allow him to have established in II iii 3, whatever he can include in the 'reason' which is incapable of supporting or opposing choices on its own, it will no longer follow that this reason cannot be the source of moral distinctions. For all that Hume's argument would now show, these distinctions might be the product of demonstration or causal inference or ordinary sense-perception and observation or some combination of these. There may, indeed, be other grounds for doubting this, but Hume's argument will now be powerless to disprove it.

But note how big a concession this would be, and how reluctant Clarke, for instance, or Butler would be to make it. Clarke insists not only that the unalterable and eternal relations of things and the consequent fitnesses are necessarily evident to the understandings of all intelligent beings – unless their understandings are very imperfect or very much depraved – but also that 'by this understanding or knowledge of the natural and necessary relations, fitnesses, and proportions of things, the *wills* likewise of all intelligent beings are constantly directed, and must needs be determined to act accordingly' unless those wills are 'corrupted by particular interest or affection, or swayed by some

54

unreasonable and prevailing passion'. And this is surely how moral characterization has been understood throughout the whole history of moral philosophy. It is not merely that it is linguistically odd to use words like 'right' and 'wrong' with no prescriptive force – to say, for example, 'X is right and Y is wrong, but of course it is entirely up to you whether you prefer what is right to what is wrong.' (If 'fair' and 'unfair', for example, are substituted for 'right' and 'wrong' here, the remark becomes more acceptable: 'fair' can more easily be used as a purely descriptive term than 'right' can.) What is more important than this linguistic point is that Clarke, Butler, and many others are concerned to defend the metaphysical view which is represented by the way in which such moral terms combine a descriptive logic with a prescriptive force, namely that there are objective requirements or categorical imperatives in the nature of things.[4] Harrison's suggestion would abandon this claim; it would save the objectivity of moral distinctions from Hume's attack only by giving up their prescriptivity. Instead of a sentiment of the understanding or a perception of the heart, we should have a straightforward perception of the understanding and, quite distinct from this, a sentiment of the heart which may or may not be associated with it.

Besides this main argument, Hume uses a number of others to show that morality is not based on reason. A second, which also echoes II iii 3, is that since passions, volitions, and actions are 'original facts and realities, compleat in themselves' – with no representative function – they cannot be true or false, and hence cannot 'derive their merit from conformity to reason'. This ignores Wollaston's argument that actions, at least, can have a representative function; but even apart from this it would show only that the morality of these various sorts of item cannot consist in conformity to reason in one very simple and literal sense, that their moral quality cannot be just truth or validity. It would not show that there is any incoherence in the notion of an objectively authoritative prescription, and so it would leave open the possibility that actions might conform, or fail to conform, to reason by obeying or violating such a prescription.

A third argument starts from the concessions Hume has made, that actions and passions can be contrary to reason in a loose sense either if they are based on a false belief about the existence or the quality of an object or if they rely upon mistaken causal beliefs and expectations. Possible examples would be running away from an imaginary danger, refusing food because you think, wrongly, that it will have a nasty taste, or trying to transmute lead into gold. But no irrationalities of any of these sorts can be what makes actions morally wrong, Hume argues, because such mistakes of fact are not held to be criminal, and people who make them are not blamed but pitied.

Fourthly, Hume echoes an argument which Hutcheson had used against Wollaston. If the rightness and wrongness of actions consisted in truth and falsehood respectively, then all wrong actions would be equally wrong; there are no degrees of falsehood. Wollaston says that there are different degrees of importance in the truths which actions may deny; but Hutcheson rightly replies that there can be differences of importance between truths only if there is some ground of moral values other than truth and falsity themselves (368). Hume extends this into an argument to show that moral distinctions cannot even be derived from truth and falsehood, adding (rather unconvincingly) that if they were so derived, not only could there be no differences of importance, but we should also be unable to distinguish morally between avoidable and unavoidable errors. Hume's argument is not as cogent as Hutcheson's simpler one, directed specifically against Wollaston's view.

Fifthly, if it is suggested that though mistakes of fact do not produce immorality, mistakes of right may do so, Hume replies, soundly, that such mistakes cannot be the *foundation* of moral distinctions; there can be a mistake of right only if there already is, for some other reason, a difference between right and wrong.

In a sixth argument Hume replies explicitly to Wollaston, interpreting his thesis, that a wrong action is one which denies things to be as they are, as meaning that an action is wrong if and only if it communicates a falsehood, if it tends to cause false beliefs. If all that was wrong with committing adultery with my neighbour's wife was that it tended to arouse, in simple-minded observers, the belief that the lady was my own wife, then, Hume says, 'if I had used the precaution of shutting the windows, while I indulg'd myself in those liberties with my neighbour's wife, I should have been guilty of no immorality.' This would be a good reply to Wollaston's theory as Hume interprets it. But it is an unfair interpretation. Wollaston identifies wrongness with an action's *declaring* that things are otherwise than they are, not with its *communicating* this falsehood. His system is indeed open to conclusive objections, but Hume's is not one of them.

Seventhly, Hume argues against Locke's or Clarke's claim that morality is susceptible of demonstration. Demonstration, he says, depends wholly on relations of four sorts: resemblance, contrariety, degrees in quality, and proportions in quantity and number. Clearly moral conclusions cannot be drawn from these alone. The obvious objection is that there may be some other kind of relation which allows demonstration, but to this Hume replies forcefully with a challenge: it is up to those who say that morality is demonstrable to point out this other kind of relation. He also shows how hard it will be for anyone to take up this challenge. What is, say, morally wrong is a certain intended action, an item which already involves a relation between the agent's mental processes and external objects; nothing that involves either only mental processes or only external objects and events can be immoral. What sort of relation could it be, Hume asks, that must thus have a foot in both camps, both in the agent's mind and in the external world, and that could not occur in either sphere on its own? Moreover, this supposed kind of relation is alleged necessarily to direct the will of every rational being, that of God no less than that of man; what kind of relation could it be that did this? Besides, Hume claims to have shown, in Book I of the *Treatise*, that there is no genuinely necessary connection between causes and effects, that is, no possibility of *a priori* knowledge that one thing will produce another. The connection between the supposed moral relation and choice by any rational agent would need to be necessary and intelligible *a priori*; it would need to have just those features which Hume has shown causal relations not to have.

This seventh argument has a good deal of force against the suggestion that there are demonstrable categorical imperatives. It would have much less force against an opponent who adopted Harrison's above-mentioned proposal, giving up any claim to objective prescriptivity. But, as I have said, that would itself be a major concession.

An eighth argument, which Hume offers as an illustration of points made in the seventh, is that morality cannot consist in relations between situations and actions, because relations just like those which, in human conduct, are regarded as immoral occur in animal behaviour and among inanimate things and are not there thought to be immoral. It is wicked for a child to kill his parent; it is not wicked if a young oak tree overtops and destroys the parent tree from one of whose acorns it grew. Incest in humans is immoral, but exactly the same sorts of sexual relations among animals are innocent. But this argument is more picturesque than cogent. It is easy to reply that there are further elements in the human situations which make them relevantly different from the non-human ones with which Hume compares them.

Many of these arguments have been directed primarily or even wholly against the view that moral judgments are demonstrable. But Hume ends with a claim that they show also that morality does not consist 'in any *matter of fact*, which can be discover'd by the understanding'. A ninth argument offers a further proof of this conclusion. If you examine any action that is held to be vicious, such as wilful murder, all you can find in it is certain passions, motives, volitions and thoughts.

> There is no other matter of fact in the case. The vice entirely escapes you, as long as you consider the object. You never can find it, till you turn your reflexion into your own breast, and find a sentiment of disapprobation, which arises in you, towards this action. Here is a matter of fact; but 'tis the object of feeling, not of reason. It lies in yourself, not in the object. So that when you pronounce any action or character to be vicious, you mean nothing, but that from the constitution of your nature you have a feeling or sentiment of blame from the contemplation of it. Vice and virtue, therefore, may be compar'd to sounds, colours, heat and cold, which, according to modern philosophy, are not qualities in objects, but perceptions in the mind. ...

These remarks combine a negative and a positive thesis. The negative one is that a moral judgment, say, that a certain action is wicked, is not a description of any empirical features of the object – in particular, the intentional action – about which it is made. The vice escapes you, presumably, because the cluster of features which you can find in the action as intended do not amount to *vice*, to anything that necessarily calls for condemnation. This seems correct. The positive thesis is that this judgment is a report that the speaker has a feeling of blame directed towards the action when he contemplates it. But this is implausible. There is a difficulty (which Reid later exploits) about what a mere *feeling* of blame might be: anything we can recognize as blaming involves judgment as well as feeling. But also, when any ordinary person calls an action vicious, he surely does not *mean* merely that it is such as to provoke in him the reaction (whatever it may be) called blaming, just because of 'the constitution of his nature', because he happens to have a certain make-up. To give Hume a defensible view here, we must read him as intending to say that this is what you ought to mean, because that is all that, on reflection, you could maintain. His analogy with secondary qualities in the modern – that is, Lockean – philosophy would support this reading. For, as Locke explicitly says, when we call something blue we do not ordinarily mean merely that it is such as to produce a certain colour sensation in us. That is all that is defensible, and so it is all that, on reflection, we ought to mean; but in practice we are 'forward to imagine that [ideas of secondary qualities] are resemblances of something really existing in the objects themselves' (*Essay* II viii 25). And the same is surely true of the wickedness that we ascribe, for example, to wilful murder.[5]

However, even if we accept Hume's negative thesis, we are not thereby forced to accept even this improved version of his positive thesis. Perhaps the only relevant matter of fact, over and above the cluster of features which, as we agreed above, do not amount to vice, is this sentiment of blaming. But the moral judgment need not be identified with the report that there is such a sentiment, for it need not be a report of any matter of fact, any more than it is a report of any relation of ideas. It could be something non-descriptive, non-cognitive, perhaps an expression of an emotion or a prescription made or endorsed by the person who makes the judgment. I think, indeed, that to say that this is what any ordinary person means when he makes a moral statement is almost as implausible as Hume's explicitly stated view that such a person means merely that the object is such as to provoke his disapprobation. But such an expression of emotion or a prescription or a combination of the two is something that we might defensibly mean. As a conceptual reform this would be a viable alternative to the one Hume seems to think necessary.

In this section, then, Hume has not only put forward quite a number of arguments which have varying degrees of cogency, he has also used them to support several different theses which are disguised within the dictum that moral distinctions are not derived from reason. Let us try to bring some order into this confusing situation.

The whole discussion is carried on subject to the assumption that the moral judgments in question are capable by themselves of directing or restraining or influencing actions. There are then six negative theses, listed below in order of (roughly) increasing strength, each of which Hume seems somewhere to be asserting.

1. Moral judgments are not demonstrable *a priori*.
2. Moral wrongness is not a matter of falsity, mistake, or bad reasoning, nor is moral rightness a matter of the opposite of these.
3. Moral judgments do not state any ordinary empirical truths. (The conjunction of 1, 2, and 3 still leaves it open that moral judgments might state truths of a special sort; moral qualities might be in effect a further set of primary qualities, discovered by a special moral sense.)

4   Moral judgments do not report *any* empirical truths about the actions (in themselves, and in their situations) about which they are made. (The conjunction of 1, 2, and 4 leaves it open that they do – or, again, that they should, in order to be defensible – state that these actions are such as to provoke certain feelings in the moral judge.)

5   Moral judgments do not express any knowledge or true beliefs.

6   Moral judgments do not express any beliefs at all. (This implies that they express something other than beliefs, perhaps that they express – but do not report – the judge's feelings, or prescriptions which he endorses.)[6]

The various arguments that I have numbered and summarized are related as follows to these six negative theses. The first argument, interpreted as using the strong premiss taken from II iii 3, that knowledge, beliefs, and reasoning (of any kind) cannot influence actions on their own, would support 6, and *a fortiori* all the other negative theses. But this strong premiss is not established by II iii 3, and is pretty clearly false. So the argument, thus interpreted, proves nothing. Alternatively, if it is taken as using the weaker premiss that no combination of demonstrative reasoning and ordinary factual and causal knowledge can by itself influence actions, this argument gives strong support to 1, 2, and 3. The second and third arguments give support only to 2. The fourth argument attempts to support 2, but it is not very strong; the fifth successfully defends 2 against a possible objection. The sixth argument is intended to support 1 and 2 by refuting Wollaston's theory, but since it rests on a misinterpretation of Wollaston it disposes only of an objection which nobody has made, and is valuable only as light relief. The seventh argument is a forceful though not absolutely conclusive defence of 1, highlighting implausibilities in anything like Clarke's theory. The eighth argument is intended to support both 1 and 3, but it is only picturesque, not cogent. The ninth argument gives real support to 3.

What emerges from this summary is that after we have discarded the weak arguments, the remainder give considerable support to 1, 2, and 3, but not to 4, 5, or 6. We can conclude that moral judgments (always on the assumption that they are intended to be intrinsically action-guiding) are not demonstrable *a priori*, are not a matter of truth and falsehood, and do not report any ordinary empirical truths. If we regard these points as established, we may find other arguments, not given by Hume, in favour of 4. These would rest upon the sheer implausibility of the objectivist view of moral sense which 3 left open, of the notion of moral qualities as analogous to the primary qualities but with a peculiar prescriptive force – G. E. Moore's 'non-natural qualities'. Then if we add the evident falsity, as an analysis of ordinary moral judgments, of the view (at times endorsed by Hume himself) that such statements say only that the action judged is of such a kind as to provoke certain feelings in the judge, then we can go on to infer 5. But no real support has been provided, nor can any be readily supplied, for 6, the rejection of all cognitivist *analyses* of moral judgments. As an account of the ordinary meaning of moral judgments, 6 seems to be false; but once 5 is established and it is admitted that moral judgments do not express any knowledge or true beliefs, 6 may become attractive as a conceptual reform.

We also noted that, as Harrison says, Hume's first argument can be evaded if the basic assumption that moral judgments can by themselves direct actions is given up. But 1, 2, and 3 would still be supported by other arguments. However, 4 would then be less cogent: *sui generis* moral qualities or relations would be more acceptable if they did not have to carry categorical imperatives with them. And then, without 4, we could not go on to 5. But the kind of moral objectivism that would thus be left open would not have appealed to Clarke, for example, or to Butler, and it would be a significant change from much ordinary moral belief.

It may seem strange that I have not yet mentioned the best known argument in this section, the passage about 'is' and 'ought'. But this passage is plainly an afterthought for Hume himself. It says that writers on morality regularly start by making various is-statements, observations about human affairs, the existence of a god, and so on, and then suddenly switch to statements whose copula is 'ought' or 'ought not'. This transition, he says, should not be made surreptitiously: 'ought' and 'ought not' express some new relation which should be explained. He finds it inconceivable that this new relation should be deducible from others which are entirely different from it; but at least, he says, it is up to the author to explain the move. Though the point is expressed rather mildly and ironically, this has been taken as the assertion of a general principle – 'Hume's Law' – that it is impossible to derive 'ought' from 'is', that is, to infer an ought-statement from any number of is-statements.[7]

Though he throws it in as an afterthought, Hume clearly regarded the point as an important one; attention to it, he says, 'would subvert all the vulgar systems of morality, and let us see, that the distinction of vice and

61

virtue is not founded merely on the relations of objects, nor is perceiv'd by reason'.

The demand that the transition from *is* to *ought* should be explained and not made surreptitiously is, of course, a fair one. And it is not, as someone might object, self-refuting: the 'should' here is very easily explained as indicating what is a necessary means to clear thinking and sound argument in the moral field. Also, the charge that the transition is often made surreptitiously is correct. But the stronger claim that *ought* cannot be derived from *is* is controversial.[8]

First, ought-statements are often hypothetical imperatives (like the should-statement above) and follow from causal statements. If doing X is the only means that is open to you to the bringing about of Y, then you ought to do X – indeed, you must do X – if you want Y. To say this is only to draw attention to the causal situation, looking at it from the point of view of someone who wants Y. Secondly there is no difficulty in deriving an ought-conclusion from premises which are all explicitly is-statements, but one of which contains a term whose meaning includes an *ought*. 'It would be wrong for you not to do X' entails 'You ought to do X', because there is an *ought* implicit in the word 'wrong'. Thirdly there are facts about ordinary language and our established conceptual scheme such as those exploited in John Searle's derivation of an *ought* from an *is*: it is one part of the meaning of the word 'promise' that someone who says 'I promise ...' in appropriate circumstances *has* promised, and it is another part of its meaning that someone who has promised to do something ought to fulfil his promise when the time for fulfilment, or the specified occasion, arrives. So, working within this conceptual scheme, relying on the multiplicity of rules associated with this part of ordinary language, we can derive an ought-statement from a set of is-statements. We shall be unable to resist this derivation if we use the word 'promise' with all its conventional meaning-links. And there will be other cases which have the same general logical structure.

When we have allowed for everything of these sorts, what have we left of Hume's Law? The thesis that remains unshaken is that an ought-statement which expresses a categorical imperative cannot be validly derived by ordinary, general, logic – by deductively valid reasoning – from any set of premises, each of which is either a logical or mathematical truth or an ordinary empirical (including causal) statement; the apparent exceptions rely on clusters of linguistic rules which, as clusters, implicitly incorporate categorical imperatives. In fact this is just negative thesis 3 again. But the remarks about *is* and *ought* do not give any further argument for this thesis. They are only a dramatic restatement of it, and the support for it must be found (as it can be found) either in the previous arguments or in the effective criticism of the apparent exceptions.

If this is the defensible form of Hume's Law, does it subvert all the vulgar systems of morality? It subverts the claim of Locke and Clarke that morality is demonstrable, and Butler's theory, in so far as he endorses Clarke's claim. Most importantly, it subverts all the systems — and they are still to be found today, as they were in Hume's time — which smuggle in a suggestion of objectively authoritative prescriptions without making it clear where they come from. But, like thesis 3 which it restates, Hume's Law leaves open the possibility that there should be objectively prescriptive moral truths or valid principles, some of which are discovered by a moral sense or by a faculty of moral intuition. This is the possibility which, as I said in chapter III, had not been excluded by the discussion in II iii 3, and was therefore still in play as a rival to Hume's psychology of action. It is this that thesis 4 would exclude; but the move from 3 to 4, though plausible, is still disputable. Hume's Law also leaves open the possibility of morality as a system of objectively valid hypothetical imperatives, or again of a system of objective values without intrinsic prescriptivity.

We must in the end admit, therefore, that though III i 1 is an extremely important contribution to moral epistemology, it is neither as neat nor as conclusive as it initially seems to be. Along with some further arguments, it can contribute to a pretty strong case against the view that there are objective moral values or principles of a categorically imperative sort. But the crucial question is still whether we can find some better explanation of the very widespread and persistent tradition of thought of which that view is a philosophical formulation. I believe that it is a great merit of Hume's theory of the artificial virtues that it contains the core of such an explanation, and therefore makes up for the inconclusiveness of his discussion of moral epistemology in part i of Book III.

V

VARIANTS OF SENTIMENTALISM

(*TREATISE* III i 2)

Hume's account of the true basis of moral distinctions is much shorter than his proof that they are not derived from reason, but it contains similar and related indeterminacies. Yet there is no indeterminacy or lack of clarity about the main point he is making. This is that the essential fact of the matter, when virtue is distinguished from vice, or right actions from wrong, is simply that people have different feelings or sentiments with regard to them. This main point is expressed in various ways.

> You can never find [the vice], till you turn your reflexion into your own breast, and find a sentiment of disapprobation, which arises in you, towards this action.

> Vice and virtue ... may be compar'd to sounds, colours, heat and cold, which ... are not qualities in objects, but perceptions in the mind.

> Morality, therefore, is more properly felt than judg'd of.

> To have the sense of virtue, is nothing but to *feel* a satisfaction of a particular kind from the contemplation of a character. The very *feeling* constitutes our praise or admiration ... We do not infer a character to be virtuous, because it pleases: But in feeling that it pleases after such a particular manner, we in effect feel that it is virtuous. The case is the same as in our judgments concerning all kinds of beauty, and tastes, and sensations.

> ... virtue is distinguished by the pleasure, and vice by the pain, that any action, sentiment or character gives us by the mere view and contemplation.

64

The pain or pleasure, which arises from the general survey or view of any action or quality of the *mind*, constitutes its vice or virtue, and gives rise to our approbation or blame, which is nothing but a fainter and more imperceptible love or hatred.

Of these all but the last come from III i 1–2; the last is from III iii 5. The same view is stated in the *Enquiry concerning the Principles of Morals*: 'The hypothesis which we embrace is plain. It maintains that morality is determined by sentiment. It defines virtue to be *whatever mental action or quality gives to a spectator the pleasing sentiment of approbation*; and vice the contrary.' Early in this *Enquiry*, when Hume is trying to present his view in a less provocative way and to say that reason has, after all, a part to play in moral determinations and conclusions, he puts it thus:

The final sentence, it is probable, which pronounces characters amiable or odious ... that which renders morality an active principle and constitutes virtue our happiness, and vice our misery: it is probable, I say, that this final sentence depends on some internal sense of feeling, which nature has made universal in the whole species. For what else can have an influence of this nature? But in order to pave the way for such a sentiment, and give a proper discernment of its object, it is often necessary ... that much reasoning should precede, that nice distinctions be made, just conclusions drawn, distant comparisons formed, complicated relations examined, and general facts fixed and ascertained.

Hume explicitly compares 'moral beauty' in this respect with beauty in 'the finer arts'; we are therefore justified in using, for example, his essay 'Of the Standard of Taste' to throw further light on his view of morality. One possible indeterminacy, therefore, can be resolved at once. Hume speaks sometimes of a moral sense, sometimes of sentiment. Though both sense and sentiment differ from reason, one would also naturally take them to differ from one another. The real trouble is that the term 'sense' is very broad: it can cover the sense-perception of primary qualities like shape or of secondary qualities like hardness or smell or sound or colour, but it can also cover sensations of pain, a sense of harmony, a sense of disgust, and a sense of outrage. But though the word 'sense' and even the phrase 'moral sense' are thus indeterminate in meaning, there is no doubt that Hume is *not* using them to say that moral awareness is analogous to the perception of a primary quality. His comparisons are constantly with secondary qualities as Locke understood them, with pain and pleasure, and with our sense of beauty or ugliness in works of art, and he makes it quite clear that he thinks that this is a matter of our having certain sentiments, feeling certain special sorts of pleasure or pain in contemplating a work of art. So even where he says 'sense', Hume means 'sentiment'.

Also, despite the passage quoted above from the *Enquiry*, he thinks of this sentiment as being essentially a feeling. Beliefs and judgments, information and reasonings, may pave the way for it, but they are not included or involved in the sentiment.

Although this problem can be decisively resolved, some others remain. It is not clear exactly what feelings or whose feelings constitute the difference, in Hume's view, between vice and virtue, or exactly what meaning he would assign to the statement (as made by any ordinary speaker) that a certain action or character is virtuous or vicious. One possibility is that 'This is virtuous (vicious)' means 'This is such as to arouse a feeling of approbation (disapprobation) in me', that is, that a typical moral judgment reports, not simply the speaker's feelings, but rather the tendency of the action or character in question to arouse certain feelings in him. But within this suggestion further distinctions can be drawn. Does such a moral statement indicate what feelings the action (etc.) now tends to arouse, or what feelings it would tend to arouse if the speaker made the 'nice distinctions' and 'distant comparisons', drew the 'just conclusions', examined the 'complicated relations', and ascertained all the relevant 'general facts' in the way Hume suggests in the *Enquiry*? Again, Hume several times suggests that a moral judgment reflects a feeling which arises from a 'general view' of the action in question, that is, the moral judge cancels those parts of his reaction which arise from the good or harm that the action (etc.) in question does to him, and compensates for its nearness or remoteness in time or place; '... we fix on some *steady* and *general* points of view; and always, in our thought, place ourselves in them, whatever may be our present situation.' He explains that we do this 'to prevent those continual *contradictions*', that is, in order to make our various moral judgments consistent with one another, to give the same moral characterization to actions and characters which are intrinsically alike, although differently related to the particular moral judge.

Another possibility is that 'This is virtuous (vicious)' means rather 'This is such as to arouse a feeling of approbation (disapprobation) in all

66

(or most) human beings', or perhaps 'in all (or most) members of the society to which the speaker belongs'. Of course within this suggestion we could again distinguish between the feelings which the action (etc.) actually tends to arouse and those which it would tend to arouse if the moral judges made all the above-mentioned distinctions and so on, and adopted a steady and general point of view. As Harrison says,[1] Hume comes close at times to the ideal observer or impartial spectator theory explicitly stated by his friend Adam Smith; a moral judgment reports or represents the feelings that an impartial spectator would have.

The contrast between these possibilities raises a further question: how uniform did Hume take people's moral judgments and sentiments to be? Throughout Book III of the *Treatise* he writes as if they were extremely uniform, once allowance has been made for nearness or remoteness, and for the good or harm an action does to the moral judge. In the *Enquiry* he speaks of 'some internal sense or feeling, which nature has made universal in the whole species'. But in 'A Dialogue' he stresses the differences between the moral views current in different societies, and in 'Of the Standard of Taste' he notes that differences of taste, both in art and in morals, really exist but are partly concealed by systematic shifts in meaning: different societies agree in approving of 'heroism' and 'prudence', but one society may include more ferocity in 'heroism' than another, or allow more cunning and fraud under the name of 'prudence'. Aesthetic, and presumably also moral, views vary not only from one society to another but also from one individual to another in the same society, and the differences are correlated to some extent with differences of age and temperament. Hume thinks that there are underlying uniform principles which somehow produce these surface variations:

> The Rhine flows north, the Rhone south; yet both spring from the *same* mountain, and are also actuated, in their opposite directions, by the *same* principle of gravity. The different inclinations of the ground, on which they run, cause all the difference of their courses. ('A Dialogue')

But this can only mean that there is a single basic psychological theory that will explain the differences of taste in art and morals, not that there is a single aesthetic theory or a single moral theory which reconciles these differences by showing that they arise only from variations in associated factual beliefs or in the range or depth of discernment of the relevant features.

Hume's various remarks cannot all be read as expressing any one of the above-mentioned views about the meaning of a typical moral statement. This is partly because he is not greatly interested in questions of meaning. But even if he had been more concerned with such questions than he was, he might not have felt bound to offer any single meaning for all ordinary moral statements. Might he not have said that 'This is virtuous' sometimes means that the action (etc.) is such as to arouse a feeling of approbation in the speaker, sometimes that it is such that it would do so if he considered it more thoroughly and/or in a more detached way, sometimes that it is such as to arouse such a feeling in an impartial spectator who is representative of the speaker's society, or of mankind in general, and so on? If either there is already a fair degree of uniformity of moral reaction, or a fair degree of uniformity is likely to be reached by deeper consideration, or by the adoption by each person of a detached or impartial point of view, and if there is a significant tendency for people to take over moral sentiments from one another, and to strive after such a general point of view, then our moral language might well be happily and usefully indeterminate between meanings of the various sorts we have been distinguishing.

But how do these various possible meanings, and the variously located actual or possible sentiments to which they refer, bear upon Hume's insistence that morality is an active principle, that it can by itself direct or influence actions, which was one of his main reasons for saying that morality is based on sentiment, not on reason? The only sentiment that could directly influence action would be one which the agent himself actually had at the time of acting. How, then, would a judgment that referred to a sentiment of the speaker, if he is not the agent, or of a representative impartial spectator, or to merely possible sentiments which one or other of these would have if he thought further in certain ways, help to direct action? Hume would have to reply that the system of interlocking, similar, and mutually supporting sentiments in a large number of people has some power to influence choices of action because each agent tends to develop sentiments like those which he thinks that others have or would have if they were better informed and more impartial. As Hume says, we not only try to make our personal moral judgments consistent with one another, we also aim at interpersonal standards. The morality that can guide action, then, is not a random collection of mere feelings, or of statements that report such stray feelings. Rather it is a system built, indeed, out of feelings but involving also people's awareness of one another's feelings, attempts to take a

68

steady and general point of view, and tendencies towards agreement in attitude.

All the possibilities we have been examining assign to typical moral statements a dispositionally descriptive meaning: they are being taken to ascribe to actions (etc.) dispositions or powers to arouse certain sentiments. But any purely descriptivist account of the meanings of moral statements seems open to this criticism: no purely descriptive statement can be action-guiding in itself, as Hume has (rightly) assumed that moral judgments are. My belief that an impartial spectator, for example, would condemn a possible action which I am contemplating will prevent me from performing it only if I also want to fit in with the spectator's system of approbation. Hume might evade this criticism by saying that what is action-guiding is *morality*, the whole system of mutually supporting and mutually modifying sentiments, not moral *statements*. But this is hard to reconcile with the most natural reading of the is-ought passage, (the reading which makes it assert Hume's Law.) For even a dispositionally descriptive statement is undeniably an is-statement, a statement of fact about certain causal tendencies, and, if a typical moral statement is to be understood in this way, then it will be an ought-statement which follows in the directest possible manner from an is-statement, namely by sameness of meaning. If Hume is to evade the criticism in the way suggested above, then we can give him a consistent position only by not finding Hume's Law in the famous passage, and reading it as saying, rather lamely, no more than it literally says, that any transition from *is* to *ought* should be explained. But in any case, typical moral statements do not seem to me to mean what any dispositionally descriptive account, or even any mixture of dispositionally descriptive accounts, says that they mean.

Such considerations may lead us to reject dispositional descriptivism. Then if we still agree with Hume's general sentimentalist thesis it will be natural to consider one or other non-descriptivist, non-cognitivist, non-propositional account of the meaning of moral statements. One such possibility is the emotivist view that the main function of a moral statement is to express, rather than to report, a sentiment which the speaker has or purports to have, and, by expressing it, to tend to communicate it, to arouse a similar sentiment with regard to the same object in a suitable hearer. Most moral predicates would, on this view, also have some descriptive meaning, but the distinctively moral element in their meaning, the part which makes Hume say that the vice escapes you until you turn your reflection into your own breast, would be just

69

this expressive and evocative force. It is easy to understand how such a system of meaning could grow up along with the growth of such an interpersonal system of moral sentiments as we have, above, supposed morality to be. Another possibility is the prescriptivist view that the main distinctive function of a moral statement is imperative, that the speaker is making or endorsing a command that the possible action which he calls right should be done, or that the one he calls wrong be not done. If this is developed, as R. M. Hare develops it, into universal prescriptivism, it says that a moral statement endorses a universalized or universalizable prescription which the speaker is implicitly applying to all actions, of himself and others, and no matter how they are related to himself, that are relevantly similar to the one about which the statement is made.[2] Such a way of speaking, too, could easily grow up in association with the above-mentioned interpersonal system of sentiments, where people strive after a steady and general point of view, and aim at both personal and interpersonal consistency. Of these two possibilities, the prescriptivist analysis plainly satisfies, in the fullest and most direct way, the requirement that moral statements should be intrinsically action-guiding. The emotivist analysis does so less directly and less completely. But the state of mind in the speaker which a statement that satisfied this analysis expressed or purported to express would be action-guiding in itself for the speaker, and the similar state of mind which it would be part of its linguistic function to arouse in a suitable hearer would likewise be action-guiding in itself for that hearer; in neither case is any further want or desire required to generate a motive, as it is with any purely descriptive statement.

Either of these two views (or some combination of them) might, therefore, have been attractive to Hume. But there is little evidence, either in III i 2 or elsewhere, that he adopted either of them. It may be, of course, that (like so many other people when they come to consider the sentimentalist explanation of morality) Hume simply failed to distinguish between expressing a sentiment and reporting it, so that those of his formulations which suggest a dispositional descriptivism may in fact reflect something closer to an emotivist view, while the remark that morality is more properly felt than judged of seems explicitly emotivist. However, I think the plain truth is that Hume was not sufficiently interested in or worried about questions of meaning to formulate clearly any such non-propositional view.

Nor is it clear that this is a defect. Though, as I have said, such non-propositional ways of speaking might well have grown up along with the interpersonal system of moral sentiments, it is, on the face of it, very strange to say that our present typical moral statements are non-propositional. They are regularly handled, both syntactically and conversationally, as if they were capable of being true or false in the same simple way as ordinary factual statements. To get a view that is plausible as an analysis of the ordinary meaning of moral statements, we should have to propose not a pure non-descriptivism but a mixed account, allowing these statements to combine emotive or prescriptive meaning, or both, with some descriptive meaning. This might be dispositionally descriptive along the lines of our previous suggestions. A moral statement might both say that an action is such as to arouse certain sentiments and either purport to express and tend to evoke similar sentiments or prescribe or forbid such actions. Alternatively, while purporting to express and tending to evoke some sentiment, or while endorsing some (perhaps universalizable) prescription, it might also describe more intrinsically the features on whose account the sentiment might be felt or the prescription issued. Such a mixed theory is not utterly implausible, because it accommodates the fact that moral statements are, on the face of it, propositional. Yet it still leaves what is distinctively moral as a non-propositional adjunct to the proposition. This does not seem to me to be correct as an analysis of ordinary meanings, though it might be attractive as a conceptual and linguistic reform.[3]

There is, however, another possible analysis of moral statements as ordinarily used. Although the only hard fact of the matter is that the speaker and others have or would have certain sentiments, that there is an interpersonal system of sentiments with regard to actions, characters, and so on, we tend to project these sentiments onto the actions or characters that arouse them, or read some sort of image of these sentiments into them, so that we think of those actions and characters as possessing, objectively and intrinsically, certain distinctively moral features; but these features are fictitious. Since these fictitious features are projections of sentiments which are intrinsically action-guiding, these features too are naturally thought of as intrinsically action-guiding. Since the system of sentiments includes a social demand that certain things be done or not done, the fictitious features are taken to involve corresponding requirements and necessities. Where the sentiment is hostility to the action and a demand that it not be done, the supposed wrongness of this action, resulting from the objectification of that sentiment, is something which in itself, if anyone were aware of it, would dissuade him from doing it. This projection or objectification is not just a trick of individual psychology. As I have said, there is a system in which the sentiments of each person both modify and reinforce those of others; the supposedly objective moral features both aid and reflect this communication of sentiments, and the whole system of thought of which the objectification, the false belief in the fictitious features, is a contributing part, flourishes partly because, as we shall see, it serves a social function.[4] I shall refer to this analysis as the objectification theory. There is at least circumstantial support for this view as an interpretation of Hume. It would agree very well with his drawing of an analogy between moral features and secondary qualities like colours, sweetness or bitterness, and so on. It would therefore make natural his retention of the term 'moral sense'. The process of projection or objectification postulated here would be an instance of the human mind's 'great propensity to spread itself on external objects' (I iii 14), and would be closely analogous to the process by which Hume explained our belief in equally fictitious necessary connections between causes and effects. There is at least one fairly explicit statement of this view, in Appendix I to the *Enquiry concerning the Principles of Morals*:

> Thus the distinct boundaries and offices of *reason* and of *taste* are easily ascertained. The former conveys the knowledge of truth and falsehood: the latter gives the sentiment of beauty and deformity, vice and virtue. The one discovers objects as they really stand in nature, without addition or diminution: the other has a productive faculty, and gilding or staining all natural objects with the colours, borrowed from internal sentiment, raises in a manner a new creation.

Another merit of this analysis, and perhaps a further reason for ascribing it to Hume, is that it is very largely correct. It seems to be the only explanation which will accommodate together (i) the fact that moral statements are regularly treated, both syntactically and conversationally, as being capable of being simply true or false – and true or false through and through, even in their distinctively moral aspect, not just with regard to a pre-moral core – (ii) the way in which these statements are taken to be intrinsically action-guiding, not only contingently upon the hearer's having certain desires or inclinations, that is, to state categorical imperatives, and (iii) the thesis, for which Hume has argued forcefully, that the essential fact of the matter, which underlies moral judgments as it does aesthetic judgments, is that people have various sentiments, or rather that there are interpersonal systems of sentiments.

72

Let us sum up the different possible views that we have been distinguishing.

1 There is a moral sense, analogous to the perception of a primary quality, though the moral quality of an action or character must somehow result from its other features, so that this 'sense' must be applied to our beliefs about the circumstances, motive, manner, and so on of the action, not directly to the action itself. The virtue (or vice) is this objective quality, detected by this special moral sense. Moral statements typically say that such a quality is found in a certain action (etc.); they are capable of being simply true or false.

2 There are, literally, no such objective features as are postulated in 1. The essential fact of the matter, when virtue and vice are distinguished, is simply that people have (and share) certain feelings or sentiments with regard to the actions (etc.) to which virtue and vice are ascribed.

For clarity, let us call 1 the objectivist or intuitionist version of moral sense, and 2 the sentimentalist version. Then I have argued that Hume's moral sense doctrine, like Hutcheson's, is unequivocally sentimentalist, not intuitionist.

Within sentimentalism we can distinguish different views about the meaning of standard moral statements.

(a) Dispositional descriptivism: the statement 'This is virtuous (vicious)' means 'This is such as to arouse a feeling of approbation (disapprobation) in X in circumstances C.' This view can be further specified, according as X is identified as the speaker, all or most members of his society, or all or most members of mankind generally, or perhaps a representative member of one of these classes, and according as C is equated with the actual circumstances or with a hypothetical situation where X has made thorough investigations, distinctions, and comparisons, and has reflected deeply, and/or is adopting a detached or impartial or universalizing point of view.

(b) Emotivism: a moral statement expresses, rather than reports, a sentiment which the speaker purports to have, and, by expressing it, tends to communicate it to a suitable hearer. This, too, can be qualified by saying that moral statements typically express sentiments that arise when someone takes a reflective and impartial point of view.

(c) Prescriptivism: in judging morally about a proposed action, a speaker is commanding or forbidding it. This is developed into Universal Prescriptivism: a moral statement endorses a universalizable prescription which the speaker is implicitly applying, or is prepared to apply, to all relevantly similar actions, irrespective of their relation to himself.

We can group (b) and (c) together as varieties of non-descriptivism. (d) The Objectification theory: the meaning of moral statements is approximately as suggested in 1 above, but the features ascribed to actions (etc.) in the distinctively moral (categorically imperative) part of these statements are fictitious, created in thought by the projection of moral sentiments onto the actions (etc.) which are the objects of those sentiments.

Hume does not explicitly discuss the choice between (a), (b), (c), and (d). There is little ground for ascribing either form of non-descriptivism to him, and much of what he says would be consistent with a (possibly acceptable) mixture of the different subdivisions of dispositional descriptivism. But there are some hints of the objectification theory, and it would fit in well with much that he does say.

As for their intrinsic merits, I think there are good reasons for not adopting the intuitionist theory. But the case against it will not be complete until we have seen how well sentimentalism can account for detailed contents of actual bodies of moral thought. No single form of dispositional descriptivism is plausible on its own; a mixture of these forms, allowing moral statements to have different meanings of this class, and many of them to be happily indeterminate between such different meanings, is more plausible; yet it does not capture the real flavour of moral judgments. Neither emotivism nor prescriptivism on its own, nor even a mixture of these two alone, is plausible, but a view combining one or both of these with the recognition of an element of descriptive meaning is not so obviously incorrect. Yet anything of this kind also leaves out something characteristic of ordinary moral statements, their claim to objectivity or authority. The objectification theory therefore seems to come closest to the truth about the central meaning of typical moral statements in ordinary use.

All the variants of sentimentalism, that is, 2 (a), (b), (c), and (d), may also be put under the heading of 'subjectivism', to contrast these with objectivism either of the intuitionist sort or of the kinds Hume is criticizing when he argues that moral distinctions are not derived from reason. But, if this term is used, we must note that it is being used here in a broad sense. We must not assimilate such kinds of sentimentalism as universal prescriptivism or the objectification theory to something that is easily refuted, the simplest and crudest form of dispositional descriptivism, that moral statements merely report what feelings their subjects tend now to arouse in the speaker.[5]

In his essay 'Of the Standard of Taste' Hume rejects the 'principle of the natural equality of tastes' and speaks repeatedly of a 'proper sentiment of beauty' and even of the 'true standard'. This might appear to be a retreat from sentimentalism or subjectivism with regard to aesthetics and, by implication, with regard to morals. But a careful reading of the essay will show that there is no retreat. The standard of beauty is still essentially a matter of sentiment. But one judgment can be preferred to another if it is freer from prejudice, based on a more accurate, practised, and delicate discernment of its object, and (especially in literature) on a better understanding of the subject and the reasoning within the work. Yet there will still be some unresolvable differences in taste, due to the different characters and passions of the critics. In fact what Hume shows in this essay is how far a theory which bases moral or aesthetic distinctions on sentiment can go in embracing what Simon Blackburn has called 'quasi-realism', how far it can, quite consistently, adopt and interpret what would seem to be objectivist ways of speaking. The fact that it can go so far constitutes a challenge to the view that a claim to objectivity is implicit in our ordinary ways of speaking – a view which, as we shall see, is urged strongly by Price and Reid, and which I have conceded in speaking about objectification. But though the possibility of quasi-realism weakens the argument to this conclusion from the typical forms and grammar of moral and aesthetic sentences, I think that direct attention to traditional ways of thinking about morality, in particular, will still detect such a claim.[6]

VI

THE ARTIFICIAL VIRTUES

1 JUSTICE AND PROPERTY (*TREATISE* III ii 1-4)

Hume concludes III i 2 with this summary: 'virtue is distinguished by
the pleasure, and vice by the pain, that any action, sentiment or
character gives us by the mere view and contemplation.' This, he says,
'reduces us to this simple question, *Why any action or sentiment upon the
general view or survey, gives a certain satisfaction or uneasiness*'. In
other words, the only remaining kind of question to be answered about
morality is the psychological or sociological one, 'Why do people
approve and disapprove as they do?' One might have thought there was
another question, 'What sorts of action or character *are* virtuous or
vicious?' In so far as this means 'What sorts are generally regarded as
virtuous or vicious?', Hume does indeed go on to answer it. But in so far
as it calls for either a report or an expression of Hume's own sentiments,
it is not answered, except that Hume shows that he is willing, on the
whole, to go along with conventional views, while enjoying the ironical
exposure of the extent to which they have been determined by mere
imagination. Hutcheson was right in saying that Hume's work lacked
warmth in the cause of virtue.

In III i 2 Hume also raises the question 'whether the sense of virtue be
natural or artificial', and foreshadows the answer that our sense of some
virtues is artificial, that of others natural. In III ii 1 he sets out to prove
that justice is an artificial virtue. As I explained in chapter I, a natural
virtue, for Hume, is a disposition which people both naturally have and
naturally approve of, while an artificial one is a disposition for which
neither of these holds; it is only by some artifice or invention that the

disposition to behave in this way has been developed, and it is only by some artifice or invention that people have come to feel approval of this behaviour and this disposition and disapproval of their contraries. By 'justice' he means primarily the sort of honesty which respects what are regarded as the rights of owners of property. He quotes the traditional definition of justice as '*a constant and perpetual will of giving every one his due*' (III ii 6), but he interprets this mainly as protecting everyone in the possession and use of what belongs to him and in the right to transfer his property voluntarily to someone else.

Hume's argument that justice is an artificial virtue is complicated and difficult, but it seems to have the following structure.

1   Any action which is virtuous is made so by its having a virtuous motive.

2   There would be a vicious circularity if the motive which thus constitutes virtue were 'regard to the virtue of the action', that is, a sense of duty.

3   So there must be an independent motive for any sort of virtuous action. What can this be in the case of honesty?

4   The motive for honest actions cannot be self-love.

5   The motive for honest actions cannot be public interest, general benevolence.

6   The motive for honest actions cannot be private benevolence or goodwill towards the person whose property rights one is respecting.

7   So there can, after all, be no motive for honest actions except regard for honesty itself.

8   Unless 'nature has establish'd a sophistry', the solution to this paradox must be that 'the sense of justice and injustice is not deriv'd from nature, but arises artificially, though necessarily from education, and human conventions.'

This is only an outline of Hume's argument. He also has more detailed reasons in support of steps 5 and 6. But the serious difficulties in it concern steps 2 and 8. What exactly is the circularity that we have to avoid? And how does the suggestion that this is an artificial virtue solve the paradox?

The further support for 5 is, first, that each separate act of justice or honesty does not, by itself, benefit the public or directly promote the general happiness; secondly, if it is objected that each separate act of honesty by its example would support the general system of rules, which is beneficial, this would not provide a motive for secret acts of honesty, but they are no less virtuous than open ones; thirdly, it is just obvious that when people are honest in ordinary ways they do not have the general happiness or public interest in mind.

The further support for 6 is, first, that one owes, and often fulfils, duties of honesty to enemies and vicious men for whom one cannot have any personal goodwill, to misers to whom the property one returns or protects can do no good, and to debauchees to whom it will rather do harm; and honesty may conflict with private benevolence towards others to whom one is much more attached. Secondly, honesty may require one to give something to, say, a rich man, where simple benevolence or charity would not require one to help him. If it is objected that benevolence does require honesty in such a case because someone is hurt more by losing what he feels belongs to him than by not receiving some equal additional benefit, Hume replies that this difference results from and presupposes the notion of property rights, and so cannot provide the basic motive for honesty that is needed to explain how respect for property is a virtue in the first place. Thirdly (though this is really a restatement of the first point), one owes honesty equally to everyone, but private benevolence is and ought to be stronger towards some than towards others, and towards many, remote from oneself, it does not exist at all.

These supporting arguments are not wholly satisfactory, but they are sufficient to reinforce steps 5 and 6, which are in any case pretty plainly correct, and so is step 4. These three steps are relevant because Hume is assuming that where there is a general kind of virtue, such as honesty, displayed in many diverse particular acts, there must also be a general motive which is the disposition to be honest, distinct from any special motives which an agent may have for some honest acts but not for others. It is obvious that some pieces of honesty will accord with and be backed up by self-interest or public benevolence or private goodwill; Hume's point is that none of these can be the general motive which constitutes this virtuous disposition, honesty itself.

But why could this general motive not be the sense of duty? What is the circularity that, according to step 2, would result if we said that this general motive is 'regard to the virtue of the action'? Suppose that I repay some money that I owe to someone. Hume asks, 'What makes this action virtuous?' This question is ambiguous. It might mean 'What is so good about repaying debts? Why should this sort of behaviour, rather than, say, standing on one's head, be approved of?' Or it might mean 'What in this particular action ensures that it is really virtuous and not just apparently or superficially so?' Now Hume thinks, perhaps rightly, that the answer to this second question is that what ensures this is that the action is done from the right motive. But if this right motive were just the sense of duty, the desire to do *whatever* is right, it clearly could not also be the answer to the first question, it could not reveal what is distinctively good about honesty in debt-paying. The sense of duty *might* have made people stand on their heads. (Indeed, it actually does sometimes produce actions that are hardly less bizarre.) I think that Hume has failed to distinguish these two questions and is therefore demanding that there should be a single answer to both of them at once, and sees that 'the sense of duty' cannot be this one joint answer. But if the questions are distinguished, there seems to be no reason why 'the sense of duty' should not be the main part of the answer to the second question. The general motive for honest actions might well be simply the desire to do whatever one ought to do, together with the belief that one ought always to be honest. The answer to the first question might well be that what is good about honesty is that it is an essential part of a general scheme of behaviour which promotes the general happiness. And if we enquire further into the answer to the second question, and ask why people believe that one ought always to be honest, an answer consistent with Hume's principles would be that this 'belief' is really a sentiment of approval, arising partly from the knowledge, or belief in the literal sense, that this general scheme does promote the general happiness, and partly from the influence of similar sentiments in other people.

All of this is intrinsically plausible and consistent with things that Hume himself says, though he might prefer to drop from his account the desire to do whatever one ought to do. Regard for the honesty of the action could itself be the general motive for honest actions; there is no vicious circle here, since what we have an artificially cultivated regard for can be the honest pattern of behaviour, not its motive. However, if this way of resolving the paradox and avoiding the circularity threatened in 2 were offered to Hume, I think he would say that this way of looking at the matter does not undermine his argument, but explains what he says in step 8: this escape route is open only because honesty is an artificial virtue.

Let us put this in another way. Hume starts by insisting that only motives are virtuous. 'The external performance has no merit ... all virtuous actions derive their merit only from virtuous motives, and are consider'd merely as signs of those motives.' That is, he is refusing to separate the answers to the two questions distinguished above, he is assuming that what is good about any kind of virtuous action must be the very motive that makes an action a genuine example of the virtue. From this he infers that there would be a vicious circularity if the virtuous motive were regard to the virtue of the action. Arguing that there is no other appropriate motive for honesty, he concludes that 'there is here an evident sophistry and reasoning in a circle.' But how does the suggestion that honesty is an artificial virtue resolve this difficulty? Is it any easier to suppose that artifice has 'establish'd a sophistry' than that nature has done so? To make his view coherent, we must, I think, take him to be relaxing the principle that actions count as virtuous *only* in so far as they are signs of virtuous motives in the case of the artificial virtues. If, and only if, honesty is an artificial virtue, we can, as I have said, not only follow but also approve of the honest pattern of behaviour as such. As we shall see, this behaviour results from the indirect operation of self-love, and promotes the general happiness. The circularity is avoided because we can approve of the honest behaviour for this reason, and not as a sign of any particularly admirable motive.

This interpretation would give Hume a coherent view. But it must be admitted that he does not explicitly relax his principle in this way; perhaps he did merely think that what is artificial can involve a sophistry whereas what is natural cannot. But at least the contrast with a natural virtue, such as kindness, is clear; for this we could have given a single joint answer to the two questions distinguished above. It is the kindly motive that ensures that this particular action is really virtuous and not only apparently so, and it is also the kindliness which is what is good about this sort of action − it is something immediately amiable, attractive, instinctively approved of. So if honesty had been a natural virtue too, there would analogously have been a single joint answer to the two questions about it. There would have been some natural disposition to act honestly, and this would have been such as automatically to call forth approval in those who saw it at work. In principle there might have been either a special natural disposition for honesty (and an associated special approval tendency for honesty) or a derived form of some general virtuous disposition such as prudence or public spirit or private benevolence. But Hume thinks that there is in fact no such special natural disposition and special natural approval tendency for honesty, and indeed that honesty is so strange and *prima facie* pointless a behaviour pattern that there could not be an instinct of either sort. (This is a weak argument, but it is excusable, since Hume could not have known what strange and elaborate instincts many animals have been given by natural selection and evolution.) His explicit arguments are therefore intended to exclude the other possibility, that honesty might have been motivated by a derived form of some general virtuous disposition.

But this leads to another difficulty: does not his own conclusion contradict this exclusion? In calling honesty an artificial virtue, is he not giving it a rather complex derivation from prudence or public spirit or both? Attention to the character of the alleged artifice will show how Hume can resolve this difficulty. As we shall see, the artifice consists in the cultivation of a sentiment in favour of every act that honesty requires, including those that are not beneficial to the agent or to the public or perhaps to anyone. It is true that the explanation of the origin of this sentiment entails that the general scheme or system of rules and practices which it supports is beneficial not only to mankind in general but also to each agent on his own. But only the general scheme. At one point Hume says that the essential difference between the natural virtues and justice is

> that the good, which results from the former, arises from every single act, and is the object of some natural passion: Whereas a single act of justice, consider'd in itself, may often be contrary to the public good; and 'tis only the concurrence of mankind, in a general scheme or system of action, which is advantageous. (III iii 1)

I think he would say that this makes it impossible that the motive for justice or honesty should be even a derived form of, for example, general benevolence; that is why an artifice is needed to introduce it. For single acts of justice taken on their own there is often *no* intelligible motive; they can be understood only as parts of a general scheme. This fact, that the explanation has to go by way of the general scheme, that this scheme cannot be understood as the sum of a large number of acts each of which could be explained and could have arisen separately, is an important part of Hume's concept of an artificial virtue.

His argument, then, though difficult, is not incoherent. Yet as an argument it is not watertight: there could have been instincts both to act honestly and to approve of honesty, that is to engage in such strange practices as not merely leaving others in possession of goods they have acquired but also repaying debts and the like. Either God or natural selection might have given us such instincts, and done so because the general scheme of which they form part is beneficial in that it enables men to live together in social groups. But though his argument is therefore not completely cogent, Hume's conclusion is probably right. We do not seem to have such instincts. As he says in III ii 2, 'our natural uncultivated ideas of morality' – that is, any instinctive morality we may have – encourage partial affections for family and friends, not the impartial and universal rules of honesty and justice, and do not involve property concepts. Whatever evolution has been at work in developing our sentiments in favour of what Hume means by 'justice' has been not biological but rather social evolution.

Before leaving III ii 1, we may well reflect how Hume's sceptical temper has led him to make a significant advance in thought. Whereas Locke and many others thought that there is a natural law of property to be found out by reason, and Clarke thought that honesty is evidently more fitting than dishonesty, and Wollaston thought that to invade property rights is implicitly to deny that things are as they are, and even Hutcheson thought that the rules of justice are easily covered by the general notion of benevolence, Hume had the sharpness of mind to see how odd and initially inexplicable the ordinarily established rules and practices about property are, and how much they are in need of some further, more elaborate, explanation, which essentially involves interrelations within a general scheme. This is the real insight summed up in the phrase 'artificial virtue'. Those who came closest to anticipating this insight were other sceptically inclined writers like Mandeville and Hobbes. But in some ways Hume's thought is subtler than that of either of these predecessors.

Having thus argued on general grounds that justice is an artificial virtue, Hume next, in III ii 2, tries to show how the rules of justice are established by artifice and why we approve of the observance and disapprove of the neglect of them.

The advantages of the division of labour and mutual protection make it better for men to live in social groups, and sexual appetite and parental care of children create small family societies, in which those advantages are first realized and revealed. Men are not completely selfish; there is natural affection and generosity among the members of these small societies. But this fact itself tells against co-operation in any larger groups. Possessions acquired by industry and good fortune are in short supply, compared with people's wants, and they can easily be taken by one from another; so competition for possessions generates conflict. Instinctive interpersonal goodwill provides no remedy for these conflicts, just because it is differentially directed towards each person's relatives and friends. 'The remedy, then, is not deriv'd from nature, but from

82

artifice, or more properly speaking, nature provides a remedy in the judgment and understanding.' That is, people can see that they would do better if they could prevent the conflicts that arise from competition for possessions and so live harmoniously together in larger societies, and they can understand that the only effective means to this is 'a convention enter'd into by all the members of the society to bestow stability on the possession of those external goods, and leave every one in the peaceable enjoyment of what he may acquire by his fortune and industry'. This convention is not, Hume insists, a contract or promise; rather it is like the convention by which two men rowing a boat pull together, without having given any promises to one another. The convention of the stability of possessions will have grown up gradually, by people experiencing the advantages of keeping it and the disadvantages of diverging from it. The ideas of right and obligation and property emerge only as this convention becomes established. Once competition over possessions has been thus neutralized, any minor causes of conflict, such as vanity, envy, and revenge, are easily held in check.

Hume argues that by this artifice it is self-love itself, operating indirectly, that restrains the direct, competitive, expression of self-love; no other passion would be strong enough to do so. We need not dispute, therefore, about whether men are naturally good or naturally wicked; all that matters is the difference between sagacity and folly. 'For whether the passion of self-interest be esteemed vicious or virtuous, 'tis all a case; since itself alone restrains it: So that if it be virtuous, men become social by their virtue; if vicious, their vice has the same effect.' There are echoes here of both Mandeville and Hobbes.

Hume thinks that though this is an artifice it is one so obvious and so necessary that men could not have lived long without establishing it. Hobbes's state of nature is only a fiction, describing what would happen if men had their present passions but lacked the intelligence to create this convention. The golden age described by the poets is another, contrasting, fiction, showing what life would be like if nothing men needed were in short supply. It, too, is instructive, because it shows how, in these circumstances, justice would not arise because it would not be needed. Equally, if men were thoroughly and universally benevolent there would be no need for justice. These contrasts show the combination of features needed to generate the system of justice and property: selfishness and 'confined generosity' (only partial affections, self-referential altruism directed towards one's own relatives, friends, and benefactors); goods scarce in comparison with wants, and easily transferable; and sufficient intelligence to see how the conflicts these factors produce can be ended by the convention of property. If you negate the third of these, you get Hobbes's state of nature; if you negate the second, you get the golden age; if you negate the first, you get a third fiction which Hume has not spelled out, a communist utopia, which corresponds to Hobbes's description of the life of bees and ants, among whom 'the common good differeth not from the private' (80). But, Hume adds in the *Enquiry*, the scarcity of goods must not be too extreme: after a shipwreck, or in a besieged city perishing from hunger, the strict rules of justice are suspended, giving way to 'the stronger motives of necessity and self-preservation'. Justice and property will be established and maintained only where moderate scarcity, in conjunction with selfishness and confined generosity, makes them useful, makes them the device by which people's interests will on the whole be best fulfilled.

Public interest or extensive benevolence, Hume argues, cannot be the first or main source of justice, because if it were strong enough to institute justice, it would make it unnecessary. Nor could justice be based on demonstrative reason and relations of ideas; for then it would have to be eternal and immutable and universally obligatory, whereas we have seen that it depends on a conjunction of contingencies. Rather justice is based on concern both for our own and for the public interest.

Though these rules are established merely by interest (private or public) 'their connexion with interest is somewhat singular. ... A single act of justice is frequently contrary to *public interest*; and were it to stand alone, without being follow'd by other acts, may, in itself, be very prejudicial to society' – for example, if a good and beneficent man honestly 'restores a great fortune to a miser, or a seditious bigot'. Equally, single acts of justice may be harmful to the agent's private interest. Yet ' 'tis certain, that the whole plan or scheme is highly conducive, or indeed absolutely requisite, both to the support of society and to the well-being of every individual.' Each member of society indicates to all the others that he is willing to follow the scheme if the others do so too. So each act of justice becomes an example and an encouragement for others; and then, given the system to which it thus contributes, each such act is after all advantageous both to the agent and to society.

This explains why and how the rules of property and honesty are established as practices, but, Hume thinks, it is a further question '*Why we annex the idea of virtue to justice, and of vice to injustice.*' Given Hume's sentimentalism, this must mean 'Why we approve of justice and disapprove of injustice'. He answers that although interest – here, I think self-interest – is sufficient to make men accept and observe the rules that they see to be necessary for secure and harmonious coexistence, yet when societies have become larger, 'this interest is more remote', and we are tempted to follow an immediate interest at the expense of the long-range, indirect, interest we have in maintaining the system of justice. But though we may thus neglect the harm our own dishonesty would do (in the end) to ourselves, we still notice the harm that the dishonesties of others do, directly or indirectly, to us. Even injustices so remote as not to affect us still displease us, because we see them as harmful to human society in general, and we sympathize with those who are adversely affected by them.

> We partake of their uneasiness by sympathy, and as every thing, which gives uneasiness in human actions, upon the general survey, is call'd Vice, and whatever produces satisfaction, in the same manner, is denominated Virtue; this is the reason why the sense of moral good and evil follows upon justice and injustice.

Two considerations seem to be mixed up here. In the first place, our moral sentiments are, as it were, an automatic, unconscious attempt by each to keep all the others in order. But, secondly, they stem from our tendency to take, as a result of sympathy, the point of view of the impartial spectator. Thus we approve of honesty and disapprove of dishonesty largely because we see the good and harm they respectively do to people in general. Although the practices of justice arise primarily from self-interest, their moral characterization arises largely from sympathetic identification with the public interest. This account anticipates what Hume is to say later about the part played by sympathy in producing all our moral notions, including our approval of what he calls the natural virtues. It leads him to say, in the end, that 'Tho' justice be artificial, the sense of its morality is natural'; that is, we approve of it naturally, out of sympathy and benevolence, when these are linked with an understanding of the social effects of the system of justice. So he seems to make justice a half-natural virtue after all.

Hume adds that the deliberate encouragement of justice by statesmen (which Mandeville saw as the sole source of the moral virtues, 'the political offspring which flattery begot upon pride') can play a secondary role; but only a secondary role. We must first have sentiments of approval and disapproval, coming from some other source, before the politicians' talk of honourable, dishonourable, and so on could have any meaning or any effect. Similarly, private education has a secondary role: parents encourage honesty in their children because they know that 'a man is the more useful, both to himself and others, the greater the degree of probity and honour he is endow'd with'.

What Hume has thus offered is a brilliant speculative analysis. But latent within it are several problems and difficulties First, does Hume show that self-interest together with understanding is sufficient to make each man accept the system of justice, without Hobbes's device of sovereignty? Secondly, has he a plausible account of how a convention can grow up and gradually establish itself; or is what he says appropriate only to the solving of co-ordination problems, not to the solving of a problem of the prisoners' dilemma type, such as we repeatedly encounter in the relations between men in social groups? Thirdly, has Hume a coherent account of how a general plan or scheme of justice is beneficial, though particular acts of justice, considered singly, are often harmful, and does he show reasons why we should always act justly or honestly, even when our action, considered on its own, is harmful? Fourthly, are the rules of property so obvious and uniform, and must they be so inflexible, as Hume supposes? Fifthly, is Hume right in isolating competition for possessions as the prime cause of conflict, and the main problem that has to be solved if men are to live peacefully together? I shall discuss each of these in turn.

First, then, are self-interest and understanding enough to make anyone accept the system of justice? We can agree that it will be in the interest of nearly everyone that there should be some system of property-protecting conventions rather than none at all. But if we find, in answer to our fourth question, that there are alternative possible schemes, it may well be that some rival scheme is, for some agents, more in their interest than the existing one. However, since Hume largely ignored this possibility (except for some critical remarks about equality in the *Enquiry*) let us leave it aside, and also assume, as he obviously did, that the actual system of justice and property gives everyone a reasonable chance of acquiring some possessions by his industry or good fortune, and that everyone, or nearly everyone, does so, so that everyone is to some extent a beneficiary of the system of property protection. Even with these favourable assumptions, particular acts of honesty, taken on their own, will, as Hume says, often be contrary to the agent's self-interest. But there are considerations of four sorts which will tend to make it in the interest of an agent to adhere steadily to justice. One is the long-range influence of individual acts on the survival of the general scheme. A second is that deviations from the rules are likely to be punished by the law or by moral disapproval or by future distrust. The first of these can have little weight on its own: the effect of particular acts of dishonesty (some of which, of course, occur all the time) on the general scheme is too remote and too slight to outweigh the selfish advantages they may bring. The second applies only if the dishonesties become known, and not if the agent has a good chance of concealing his crimes and getting away with them. The third consideration is that the agent will hardly be able to conceal his crimes from himself (though some delinquents try hard to do so), and if he has acquired the tendency to disapprove of dishonesty he will suffer pangs of conscience. A fourth consideration is that the selective dishonesty which would evade both legal and moral sanctions is not, on the whole, practicable: if one is dishonest enough by disposition to take advantage of the cases where one can get away with it, and also to be pretty immune to the pangs of conscience, one is very likely to be dishonest in a more extensive way, and to incur the legal and moral penalties of being known to be so. Admittedly, these four sorts of consideration together do not constitute a watertight egoistic case for honesty; there will be some occasions for some agents when, despite all of them, dishonesty would pay. But Hume need not deny this. All he needs to say is that honesty will be in accordance with self-interest in a sufficiently large proportion of cases to sustain the general scheme. And this claim is plausible, given our favourable assumptions about the character of the scheme itself.

This argument does, however, presuppose that there is some system of legal sanctions. It also presupposes that people generally have annexed the idea of vice to injustice, that they have appropriate and strong sentiments of disapprobation. Without this our third consideration would not exist, nor would the moral sanctions in the second. And in practice the legal sanctions could not flourish or be effective without the support of widespread moral sentiments. So Hume is not quite right in suggesting that prudent self-interest is enough to maintain the *practice* of justice, leaving the moral characterization of it to be the work of sympathy and benevolence. These two are necessarily intertwined: the moral sentiment in favour of justice (and against injustice) is part of what commends the practice of it to self-interest. Still, this is only a complication. We can agree that once the general scheme is established its elements will support each other. Because honesty is widely approved, it will be sufficiently in the interest of a large enough number of people for it to survive as a predominant though not exceptionless pattern of behaviour; because it does so survive, it will promote the well-being of most people; and because it can be seen to promote this, it will be generally approved, partly from each person's self-interested point of view and partly through the operation of sympathy, but partly also with the help of explicit propaganda in its favour, for which there will be several motives, including the confined generosity of parents towards their children. We have here included in this explanation the ordinary machinery of a legal system, but we have not had to invoke Hobbes's device of an absolute sovereign.

Conceding that such a general scheme, once established, could be self-sustaining, we can turn to our second problem. Will Hume's notion of *convention* explain how such a scheme could come into existence, without being imposed by any authority and without any explicit social contract? We must distinguish pure co-ordination problems, where two (or more) agents have no real conflict of interests, but need to find the pattern of combined action that will be most advantageous to each separately, from partial conflict problems, where two (or more) agents have interests that agree in some respects but conflict in others. The prisoners' dilemma is a paradigm case of a partial conflict problem. (Conflict, because the payoffs to the players differ in such a way that each can gain an advantage at the expense of the other, but only partial because it is not a 'zero sum game': some possible outcomes are better than others for both players taken separately.) It is initially plausible to suggest that a convention can come into existence to solve a pure co-ordination problem, but not one of partial conflict.

This can be illustrated with Hume's own example of two men rowing a boat, which is ambiguous between these two types of problem. Is Hume thinking of two men (each with a pair of oars) each of whom has made up his mind to row, and who are agreed about where to go, so that their problem is only how to synchronize their strokes, to keep rowing in time? If so, 'convention' may be an answer. It will be to the advantage of each, if they happen to start out of time, to modify his stroke to bring it closer to synchronization with the other man's. The one who is ahead will slow down, the one who is behind will speed up. Each such adjustment will make rowing easier and more pleasant for the man who makes the adjustment as well as the other, and a series of small adjustments will soon produce nearly perfect co-ordination, and any accidental divergences from co-ordination will be corrected by the same forces. Or is Hume thinking of two men who, like our first two, are agreed about where they want to go, but each is lazy and would like the other to do all or most of the work? This is a partial conflict problem, and it is not immediately clear that a 'convention' would now bring about co-operation. However, let us fill in some details. Suppose that they both want to get across the river, and each wants this enough to make it a good bargain for him, with something to spare, if they get across by sharing the work equally, but neither is so keen to get across that it would be to his advantage to do so by doing all the work on his own. Let us also suppose that each only slightly prefers to get across sooner rather than later, and that this preference is not strong enough to make it worth his while, for this reason, to add his efforts if the other man is rowing in any case. We now have a situation of the form of a prisoners' dilemma. Each man can say to himself, 'If the other chap is going to row, I prefer not rowing to rowing, and equally if the other chap is not going to row I prefer not rowing to rowing'. It seems, therefore, that neither will row, and they will not get across the river, though it would be better for each, on his own, if they got across by sharing the work. In these circumstances they might reasonably welcome some external authority, analogous to Hobbes's sovereign, who would force them both to row. Alternatively, what would help is something that would visibly tie their actions together, so that each could believe that the other would row if and only if he did so himself. The argument from dominance, that since it is better for me not to row if you do, and also if you don't, it is sensible for me not to row, fails if your decision whether to row or not depends on mine, if by rowing myself I can encourage you to row. But an agreement or promise or contract is not the solution, because even when one has been made each man will have the same motive for breaking the agreement that he had before for not rowing, and we cannot yet assume that there is any moral sentiment to support the keeping of agreements, or, of course, any Hobbesian sovereign. In Hume's order of treatment, rules about agreements and promises come after rules about property, but in any case he is trying to explain the two independently, denying that there is any need to derive one from the other, and government is introduced still later. So we are now looking for a 'convention' that does not presuppose a moral sentiment in favour of agreement-keeping or any other enforcing authority. Surprisingly, perhaps, we can find one. Each man can say to himself, '*Perhaps* the other chap will row if and only if I do; it can do no harm to find out.' So one of them begins to row, just a little bit, without straining himself, and watches to see what the other will do. The other, in a similar experimental spirit, wondering whether his rowing too will

89

encourage the other, tries rowing gently; if the first then rewards him by rowing a bit harder, they will soon both be fully at work. But perhaps one starts to slack when the other has got going; the other notices this, and eases off at once as a warning. The slacker will then, for purely selfish reasons, put more effort into it; they can thus keep each other up to the mark. In circumstances like those outlined here, co-operation can be maintained by each party's readiness to use the sanction of non-co-operation. But this will work only if the degree of co-operation is fairly finely adjustable, if it can be turned gradually up or down in response to what the other party does. In this way, even partial conflict problems can be solved by 'convention', without explicit contract, without an external sanctioning authority, and even without any specifically moral feelings. Even if an explicit agreement is made, what maintains and enforces it may be this sort of reciprocal sanctioning rather than any respect for agreements as such. This pattern of interaction could therefore provide the foundation on which a more elaborate system involving moral sentiments might be built.

However, this analysis relies essentially on reciprocation between just two persons. Can it be extended to a many-person problem? Even with only three players, if A and B are encouraging one another by co-operating, it may suit C to be a 'free rider'; then how can A and B put pressure on C to join in the work without harming one another and weakening their own co-operation? The simple answer is that a many-person problem can be solved as above if it can be structured as a cluster of two-person games; for example, if, when C starts to deviate, A and B can reduce their degrees of co-operation *with C*, while still co-operating as before with one another. It is obvious that the problem of establishing property rules and respect for them in a community can be thus structured, so that Hume is right in thinking that it could be solved by the gradual growth of a convention.

On the other hand, we need not insist on the historical claim that property rules did grow up in just this way. The actual growth of property rights presumably involved a larger element of force and of asymmetrical relations than this account would suggest. But conventions can grow up in something like the way sketched here to regulate relations even between parties who start from unequal bargaining positions, as long as the resulting compromise is to the advantage of each as compared with his own initial position. And in any case we can regard any such speculative historical description mainly as an expository device, whose chief value is that it reveals a basic interplay of motives which can constantly underlie and maintain a system of justice.

Thirdly, can Hume coherently maintain that the general scheme of justice is beneficial, though many of the particular acts of justice or honesty which together make it up *are not* beneficial? Or can he only mean that these particular acts *would not be* beneficial if the scheme as a whole were not there, or that they *seem not to be* beneficial if one counts only their immediate effects, neglecting the value of their long-range tendency to support the scheme, but that each such act is really beneficial when the scheme is in force and the long-range tendency to support the scheme is counted? And if these particular acts literally *are not* beneficial, does the fact that the general scheme is beneficial give us reasons (based on self-interest or public spirit and general benevolence) for performing these particular non-beneficial acts?

Hume may well not have been clear about this, and may have meant that the particular acts in question actually *are* beneficial, given the existence of the system of justice and their tendency to support it, though they *are not* beneficial *apart from* their long-range tendency and *would not be* so if the system were not working. But he could have defended the stronger claim, which, though paradoxical, is not incoherent. It is perfectly possible that each single act of a set should not be beneficial, even when the others in the set are there and all its effects are taken into account, and yet that the co-occurrence of these acts should be beneficial. A simple model will show this. Suppose that in an election the candidate of the good party is elected by a majority of more than one vote, but that each single voter for this party would have done something useful if he had not spent the time going to the polling booth, but also that the sum of all these utilities is less than the utility of getting the good party's candidate elected. Then the complete set of acts of voting for this candidate rather than staying away and doing something useful is beneficial. But each act in this set is not beneficial but harmful: without it, this candidate would still have been elected, and something useful would have been done that was not done. Admittedly there would in principle have been something still more beneficial than the above-mentioned complete set, namely that just enough of these voters should have voted to elect their candidate with a majority of one, while the others did something useful instead. In that case each act of voting, as well as the set, would have been beneficial. But this may not have been a live option. Perhaps no one could have told just how many votes would be needed, and even if this had been known it might not have been possible to organize things so that just the right number voted. This is an example of a rather special sort. But something analogous to it could hold in a situation of the sort of which Hume is thinking. Perhaps it is necessary, if the general scheme of justice is to flourish, that there should be a fair number of acts of honesty whose beneficiaries are misers, debauchees, seditious bigots, and the like; but it may be that more such acts are performed than is strictly necessary for this purpose. Then each such act, given its actual setting, really does more harm than good, but the collection of them does more good than harm. Again there would in principle be something better, namely that just the right number of acts of honesty to the undeserving should be performed, but this may well not be a live option: perhaps this right number could not be ascertained, and in any case such a complex practice could not be organized.

In showing how this could happen, we have by implication also shown how there can be reasons, based on public spirit, for doing acts which individually are not beneficial. It may be that the only practicable alternatives are either to perform all the component acts of a beneficial general scheme, or to change our practice so radically that these benefits are lost. The theoretical possibility of performing just the minimum number of these acts, so as to ensure that each of them is also individually beneficial, may be just that: a theoretical possibility, not a real alternative.

The key point here is that in the actual circumstances the real unit of choice may be not a single act but a practice. Discussions in moral philosophy have often misleadingly concentrated attention on the question of the rightness of acts. Even when indirect utilitarian theories have been put forward, they have commonly been both named and presented as *rule* utilitarianism. But then they are paradoxical, for the natural way to take a rule is to think of it as guiding choices in the particular cases that fall under it, and if a real choice were open in the particular case it is hard to see why a utilitarian would not choose the most beneficial single act. But if the only effectively open choice is between practices (or, equivalently, between dispositions which will then largely *determine* choices in particular cases), then it is easy to see why one might rationally choose a practice which carries with it some acts which one would not choose in isolation. It is not that these are chosen for their effects on the general practice; they may still be non-beneficial even when any effects that can genuinely be ascribed to them are taken into account; rather they are themselves side-effects of an intelligible larger-scale choice.

This point is a logical one, and holds independently of the special motive of public spirit or general benevolence with reference to which it has been stated. For example, one may reasonably, out of prudent self-interest, adopt a regular practice and cultivate a disposition in oneself, or, again, enter into and try to maintain an interpersonal general practice with its associated dispositions, because the practice as a whole (in either case) is advantageous to oneself, although some of the separate acts which constitute it (either one's own or those of other agents) will be against one's interest. Hume does not spell out these details, but the fact that they can be spelled out shows that our third problem does not constitute a sound objection to his account.

The fourth problem is whether the rules of property are as obvious and as uniform as Hume thought, and whether they need to be so inflexible. He was surely right in saying that 'Property must be stable, and must be fix'd by general rules.' The alternatives to general rules would presumably be decisions by some authorities which were either arbitrary or based on principles so complex or insights so profound that their outcome in many particular cases would be hard to predict. Neither of these is as likely to secure the widespread acceptance needed to resolve conflicts about possessions as are fairly straightforward rules that most people can understand. But this does not mean that there is only one possible body of rules. Legal systems can restrict the kinds of property that can be held and the ways in which they can be used and transferred. Redistributive taxation may be part of the property system. Hume speaks of 'the enjoyment of such possessions as we have acquir'd by our industry and good fortune'. There is a strong case for ensuring that people do acquire what represents the real product of their industry, but it is disputable how this can be achieved. There is only a weaker case for their being able to retain what they get by good luck, so that there would be nothing against rules which gradually redistributed the products of chance, which would include inherited wealth. There is, therefore, an important question which Hume has largely ignored, of the choice between different systems of justice and property, and some systems are more likely than others to satisfy the 'favourable assumptions' that we needed in order to defend Hume with respect to the first problem discussed above. It is true that in the *Enquiry* he considers, and rejects, a possible system of enforced equality; but even if his arguments against this are good ones, it is by no means the only alternative.

The point can be illustrated by an example which, as I have said, Hume uses in the *Enquiry* for another purpose. When he says that in a besieged city the strict rules of justice are suspended, giving way to necessity and self-preservation, he refers to two different degrees of urgency. First, conditions may be so bad that men return to Hobbes's state of nature: the threat of starvation is so imminent that they cannot seriously enter into the long-range calculations needed to make them accept a system of social rules at all: the situation is seen as one of *sauve qui peut*. But, secondly, long before this stage is reached a sensibly governed besieged city will have *changed* the rules about property in food and other vital commodities. The government may have commandeered all supplies; at the least it will have insisted on disclosure of all stocks, strict rationing, and compulsory purchase where necessary. Now it may turn out that even in normal times our relation to some resources is rather like that in the besieged city; if so, there will be a case for adopting with regard to property of such kinds a set of rules very different from those that Hume takes to be obvious and universal.

Our fifth problem was whether Hume is right in isolating competition for possessions as the prime cause of conflict. A moment's reflection on the political conflicts in the modern world shows that while such competition may be the most important underlying cause of conflict, it does not operate on its own, but gets mixed up with systems of power and organization, racial and religious divisions, and so on. Opportunities for acquiring possessions are often the subject of dispute, and these are not resolved merely by having simple conventions about the stability of possessions once they are acquired and their transference by consent. Here, too, Hume has ignored important questions and so arrived at an over-optimistic conclusion.

In III ii 3 Hume discusses 'the rules, which determine property'. But he is not here raising our question about the choice between different systems of property, but rather referring to the ways in which, within the existing system, someone may acquire property. He lists particularly 'Occupation, Prescription, Accession, and Succession'. Occupation means simply taking something not yet owned by anyone, perhaps a wild animal or a desert island. Prescription is the process by which someone becomes the owner of something just by having it in his possession for a long time. Accession occurs when some new item is somehow produced by something we already own – 'the fruits of our garden, the offspring of our cattle, and the work of our slaves'. Succession is the inheritance of property, without explicit bequest, from a parent or near relation. The examples given in his footnotes show that Hume, despite his failure to prepare himself for a legal career, was writing with his law books, and particularly treatises on the Roman civil law, very much in his memory, if not open in front of him. The main thesis for which he argues here is that these accepted legal rules are not rationally determined, but are largely the work of the imagination: legal ownership is fixed by various associations of ideas, and the choice of one association rather than another is often arbitrary.

We can agree with what is in any case a corollary of his earlier arguments, that there are no *a priori* demonstrable principles for the acquisition of property. That someone is the rightful owner of some newly existing item is a matter of social rules and moral sentiments, and the only questions are 'How did the present rules and sentiments arise?' and 'Shall we keep these rules or change them?' The most interesting rivals to Hume's account would be that the present rules arise from instincts, or that they are derived from utility, or that they have been determined by those who have had power and reflect their interests. Similarly we might recommend changes either on grounds of utility or with regard to special interests which we want to promote.

In the *Enquiry* Hume argues that the rules about the acquisition of property are too complicated to be due to instinct. On the other hand he would have to admit that at least some of them are favoured by utility. The difference Hume mentions between the rights of someone who 'has hunted a hare to the last degree of weariness' and someone who is just about to pick an apple – that the hunter has, while the apple-picker has not, a legitimate grievance if someone else gets in ahead of him and grabs the hare or the apple – is readily explained by the utility of rewarding industry. The hunter has put a lot of work into making the hare available, whereas the apple-picker has not put any work into making the apple available. In the *Treatise* Hume says that even here the industry creates only an imaginative link, but in the *Enquiry* he seems more willing to ascribe the detailed rules, as well as the general system of property, to utility. Prescription could be defended in terms of the utility of making titles secure and knowable: it is a nuisance for intending buyers, for example, if someone who offers property for sale may not be its rightful owner, although he has held it for years. But prescription is also a convenient rule for those who have managed to acquire and keep possessions by however dubious a process. Since having large possessions, however acquired, and having power are likely to go together (with causation in both directions: possessions may produce power, and power may give the opportunity for questionable acquisition), this rule could also be explained as tending to the advantage of those who have had power. On the whole we should expect that the established rules would have had some such solid motivations or functions; arbitrary imaginative links are likely to have been influential only in marginal cases. But a more radical criticism of what Hume says in III ii 3 is that he has not considered the main rules which determine property. These would be the working principles of the economic system which allocate to some rather than others what are, in reality, the products of the industry of many people in complex and indirect forms of co-operation. And these, surely, are affected by the interests of those who have power of one kind or another, and hence, if this covers a wide range of interests, by some sort of utility; they can owe little to imagination and the association of ideas.

The transference of property by consent, which Hume treats briefly in III ii 4, is obviously in accordance with utility. People will exchange goods for other goods or for money only if each wants what he is getting more than what he is giving up. But Hume is happy to find imagination at work even here in some of the legal rules about the transfer of property. Where the property whose ownership is being transferred is too large or immovable to be actually handed over, the law requires that some symbol of it be literally handed over. This procedure helps people to think of ownership as a real relation or connection between the owner and the property – as if it were a rope tied to the goods, of which the owner has the other end in his hands – whereas in reality A's ownership of X is constituted simply by the fact that other people morally approve of and legally permit A's enjoyment of X, and morally disapprove of and legally forbid any interference with that enjoyment. Hume is still arguing against the view that bases morality on relations of fitness which are supposed to arise out of other real relations between things.

2   THE OBLIGATION OF PROMISES   (*TREATISE* III ii 5)

In III ii 5 Hume first argues that the obligation to keep promises cannot be explained without reference to conventions and then tries to show how it can be explained in terms of conventions. He is both proving that promise-keeping is an artificial virtue and showing why and how this artifice is constructed.

A promise would not be intelligible antecedently to human conventions; men 'unacquainted with society' could not enter into agreements with one another, even if they could perceive each other's thoughts. Promising would be naturally (pre-socially) intelligible only if there were an act of the mind which it expresses, but Hume easily shows that neither resolving nor desiring nor willing the action is the same as promising. If there were an act of the mind here, it would have to be *the willing of the obligation*, and this is indeed what we suppose a promise to be. It is thought of as the voluntary taking on of an obligation to do something, where that obligation was not previously in force.

But, Hume argues, this is absurd. Since (in view of the sentimentalism he has already defended) an obligation consists simply in various feelings of approval and disapproval, and we cannot merely by willing change our own, or anyone else's, feelings, we cannot will that there should be a new obligation, or create one by willing this. He adds (in a footnote) that this would still follow even if morality consisted in relations and were discoverable *a priori* by reason; for merely willing could not change any relations. If it is objected that the willing, being a new object itself, would introduce the new relations into which it entered, Hume replies that this would involve a circularity: the willing would have to be the willing *that it itself and its relations should be there*.

He also echoes and applies here his general argument (given in III ii 1) to prove that justice is an artificial virtue. For any action required as a duty, there must be a motive in human nature capable of producing the action, and this cannot, he thinks, on pain of circularity, be just the sense of duty itself; but there is no such motive for promise-keeping other than the sense of duty with the belief that one ought to keep promises. I have already discussed this argument as originally presented, and I shall not go over it again. But it is clear that he must mean that there is no motive for promise-keeping other than the sense of duty prior to the establishment of conventions. It is this that would prove it to be an artificial virtue, and Hume will go on to show that a convention can arise which creates a motive of self-interest in favour of promise-keeping.

Hume is here arguing against two views, each of which would be a rival to his own account of promise-keeping as an artificial virtue. One of these suggests that one can somehow create an obligation just by deciding to do so. The other regards fidelity to promises as a natural virtue, implying that we have some natural tendency (either directly, or by derivation from benevolence) to keep faith, and that we either have a further natural tendency to approve of this or can perceive rationally that we ought to do so.

A simple variant of the first view is stated by Hobbes both in *Leviathan* and, more clearly, in *De Corpore Politico* (59, 102). Since to promise is to will to do something at a future time, and not to do it involves willing not to do it, someone who breaks a promise is contradicting himself, willing both to do and not to do the same thing. But it is easy to reply that all that happens is that he wills at t_1 to do X at t_2, but wills at t_2 not to do X at t_2; that is, he changes his mind, and there is nothing absurd about that. But subtler variants of this line of thought have been put forward by E. F. Carritt and John Searle.[1]

The core both of Carritt's argument and of Searle's is that 'I promise' means 'I hereby place myself under an obligation.' Carritt suggests that this statement (presumably when used in appropriate circumstances) is self-verifying and therefore cannot be false: if anyone succeeds in making a promise, then he *has* placed himself under an obligation, for that is what promising is. But can an obligation be thus conjured out of thin air? Any inclination we may have to believe that it can will fade out when we reflect on the formally analogous attempt to impose an obligation on someone else simply by saying to him 'I hereby place you under an obligation', or by using some word or phrase that is defined as meaning this. Only someone who endorses the institution of promising, or its other-directed analogue, will say that, as a result of this performance, someone is under an obligation.[2]

It might be objected that the reason why I cannot place someone else under an obligation just by saying so is that I am not in authority over him. If in some special case I am in authority over someone else, I can place him under an obligation in this way, and promising works because I am always in authority over myself. But this reply only brings out the point of the criticism. To see either performance as creating an obligation, we must presuppose a more basic moral principle which gives the obligation-creator this authority. In the case of promising, it is the authority of me-as-I-am-now to bind me-as-I-will-be. Even the supposed absolute identity of a person will not entail this; for why should the identity not work equally well in the reverse direction, giving me-as-I-will-be the authority to invalidate any undesired acts of me-as-I-am-now?

Searle's treatment of promising as a speech-act throws some light on the otherwise obscure notion which Hume has mentioned but rejected, that promising is a special 'act of the mind'. In an explicit performative the speaker does something by saying that he does it; analogously in the supposed act of the mind one would do something by willing to do it. But there could be an act of either sort only if there were already an institution of promising, and although Searle's derivation of an *ought* from an *is* goes through, given a certain body of linguistic rules attached to the word 'promise', to accept this whole body of rules is in effect to endorse the institution of promising. So the crucial question is, 'what gives rise to that institution, and to our endorsement of it?'. This is the question that Hume's own account is to answer, and that account cannot be made redundant by any considerations about the very meaning of the term 'promise' or the mere notion of laying oneself under an obligation.

Hume is also right in denying that fidelity to promises is a natural virtue. There could hardly be direct instinctive support for something so dependent on a rather advanced use of language, and there is no way of deriving it as a requirement of benevolence without showing how it works in social intercourse as part of a convention. Richard Price (as we shall see) claimed to be able to perceive its obligatoriness directly, as a special case of veracity, but the obligation to keep a promise is stronger than the obligation to speak the truth.

Later in this section Hume adds further arguments to prove that promises and the obligation to keep them cannot be understood in terms of any private act of the mind. To come into force, a promise must be expressed by words or signs; it must be made *to* someone; and if a promise is so expressed, then, provided that the promiser knows the meaning of what he says, he is bound by it, even if he has a private intention not to fulfil it, which would cancel the supposed act of the mind. Promising is essentially an interpersonal performance, and the obligatoriness must arise somehow out of this.

Promising, Hume says, is based on the necessities and interests of society, in view of the same aspects of human nature as were invoked to explain the origin of property. Men are selfish, or have only 'confin'd generosity', so they will not do anything for strangers except for a reciprocal advantage, in an exchange of goods and services. But unless the mutually aiding performances were simultaneous, the one who did his bit first would have no good reason to expect that the other would do his bit in return at all; and, realizing this, the first man would not do his bit either. Non-simultaneous reciprocity would often be of advantage to both parties, if it could be arranged, but purely selfish individuals are, *prima facie*, unable to arrange it. This is the problem that promises and agreements and contracts exist in order to solve. But how do they solve it? Essentially by a convention of the same sort that was illustrated by our two rowers in a state of partial conflict.

> I learn to do a service for another, without bearing him any real
> kindness, because I forsee, that he will return my service, in

expectation of another of the same kind, and in order to maintain the same correspondence of good offices with me or with others. And accordingly, after I have serv'd him, and he is in possession of the advantage arising from my action, he is induc'd to perform his part, as foreseeing the consequences of his refusal.

In other words, when someone promises to do something tomorrow, it is as if he were doing tomorrow's action today; he is able to exchange it for a present benefit. And his primary motive for fulfilling the promise tomorrow is the hope of being able to make similar beneficial exchanges in the future.

This explanation is sound, but it rests upon several presuppositions. One is that the same two people are likely to be repeatedly in situations where they can, to the advantage of each, engage in non-simultaneous reciprocal services or exchanges of goods. The prospect of future beneficial agreements is the sanction for the fulfilment of the present one, and it is the first performer's knowledge that the second performer is exposed to this sanction that gives him a reason for performing first. A second assumption is that it is common knowledge among those involved that people's behaviour is governed by fairly stable dispositions, so that anyone who fulfils one agreement is reasonably thought likely to fulfil another, and anyone who breaks one is reasonably thought likely to break another. A third is that people will remember one another's behaviour, and both bear a grudge against someone who defaults on an agreement and distrust him in the future.

 This third necessary assumption suggests that we cannot sharply separate the practice from the moral approval, and explain the former in terms of self-interest alone. Strictly speaking, however, this case is analogous to that of honesty about property. We can describe how self-interest, combined only with plausible non-moral psychological assumptions, could by way of a convention supported by mutual sanctioning give rise to a basic practice – here that of agreement-keeping, as there that of not taking the possessions of others. But this practice grows into the full system of property rights in the one case and promising in the other, with the full advantages of each, only when the basic practice is reinforced by moral feelings. The circularity which Hume was concerned to avoid is avoided just because the basic practice can exist first to be the object of the incipient moral sentiment. 'Afterwards', he says, 'a sentiment of morals concurs with interest, and becomes a new obligation upon mankind', and he adds that '*Public interest, education,* and *the artifices of politicians'* have the same effect here as with honesty. In the full system of promising the moral sentiment and indeed the concept, which was initially so puzzling, of placing oneself under an obligation, play a part and help to explain why promise-keeping accords with self-interest. The self-interested case for keeping promises is made stronger and applies more widely because people have, and are known to have, moral attitudes as well as stable dispositions.

This last point entails also that Hume's explanation can show why people have a tendency to keep promises, and to disapprove of breaking them, even in cases where it is not advantageous to the promiser to do so. The full working of the system requires that the very fact that I have promised to do something should be felt to give me a reason for doing it, in itself and apart from any explicit self-interested calculation. Dispositions, whether of behaviour or of approval and disapproval, cannot be quickly switched on and off. While the convention of agreement-keeping will grow up largely because it is advantageous, in the central cases, to each party to do his bit, in reliance on the other, and to fulfil his undertaking when it falls due, these advantages themselves presuppose that choices are not isolated, but follow fairly regular patterns, and moral feeling about agreement-keeping and agreement-breaking as kinds of conduct adds to the assurance of this regularity. There will, therefore, be no live option of fulfilling all and only those agreements which, taken in isolation, it is in the long-term interest of the promiser to fulfil. People in general, and each agent on his own, will be able to get the full and very real advantages of a system of promise-keeping only by developing a tendency to keep all promises and to disapprove of all violations of them. (Though this can be qualified by the recognition that agreements are of varying degrees of bindingness, and that some, at least, can be overruled by considerations from elsewhere in the moral system.)

One objection that might be raised is this. Do not the tendency to feel and show gratitude, and the related tendency to approve of gratitude and to condemn ingratitude, fulfil much the same social function as promising? Do not these (in conjunction with the converse tendency to bear a grudge against those who do one harm or who fail to show gratitude for benefits) also enable people who are primarily selfish or equipped only with confined generosity to do things for one another at some initial cost to the agent, and so to achieve non-simultaneous reciprocal benefits? And if the simpler mechanism of gratitude and grudge-bearing (which could well be instinctive, and so constitute a natural virtue) would do the trick, what need is there for the more elaborate and more obviously artificial convention of promising and promise-keeping? And then, if it is not needed, promising can hardly be explained by its alleged social function.

I suggest, however, that gratitude and promise-keeping perform slightly different though admittedly similar functions. Hobbes included both in his list of the 'laws of nature', that is, theorems about the means to peace and self-preservation. Where the benefits that one person confers on another are great in comparison with the cost to the conferrer, but the occasions for them occur randomly and irregularly, it will be to each person's advantage to maintain a number of bonds of gratitude. Repeatedly helping others who are disposed to be grateful will be a good long-term investment, even though one cannot tell just when it will pay off. But where the cost to A of helping B is only a little less than the advantage this gives to B, and vice versa, each person will need to be able to foresee a fairly equal reciprocal benefit before he is willing to bear the cost of helping the other. In these circumstances general bonds of gratitude are not likely to be established, because they would not make it a sufficiently good bargain to help someone else. But reliable promises would achieve this. They ensure a quick and calculable return on the investment. The bonds of gratitude or reciprocal altruism are one variant of confined generosity; but the making and keeping of promises make possible reciprocal benefits even where confined generosity of any sort is lacking.

As Hume points out, we shall need signs – and verbal signs are the most plainly effective ones – to mark off the special cases where one makes or exacts a promise from those where people help each other out of simple goodwill or gratitude or the expectation of gratitude. We need a distinctive language of promising.

But Hume says two different things about the use of the language of promising. One is that 'After these signs are instituted, whoever uses them is immediately bound by his interest to execute his engagements, and must never expect to be trusted any more, if he refuses to perform what he promis'd.' That is, this use of language is just part of the convention, and the main motive which establishes and maintains this convention is indirect self-interest. The other remark is that

we cannot readily conceive how the making use of a certain form of words shou'd be able to cause any material difference. Here, therefore,

we *feign* a new act of the mind, which we call the *willing* an
obligation; and on this we suppose the morality to depend.

Now perhaps some philosophers have introduced such a fiction. But
there is no need to suppose that this fiction is in general an integral part
of the process of promising. Given the reasons why a convention is
needed and is likely to grow up, we can see how something that we may
call willing an obligation is part of the conventional practice – a real, not
a fictional, part. The obligation will consist (in accordance with the
sentimentalist theory) in the sentiments felt by the promiser and by
others in favour of keeping agreements and, especially, against breaking
them. And although, as Hume says, one cannot directly will sentiments
into existence, once I know that I myself and others are in general
disposed to condemn agreement-breaking, I can (out of intelligent self-
interest, for reasons already given) *voluntarily do what will expose me to
such condemnation if I then break my agreement.* Is not this willing
myself to be under an obligation? There would be a fiction here only if
some such act of will were supposed to create the obligation on its own,
by some purely logical trick, without the complex apparatus of the
convention and the desires, beliefs, sentiments, and expectations which
maintain it.

In Hume's theory of fidelity to promises as an artificial virtue, three
distinct claims are mixed up together. The first is that promising is
something essentially *social*, not understandable or explainable in terms
of anything that could be true of an individual on his own. The second is
that it is *conventional*, that neither the keeping of promises nor the
disapproval of promise-breaking is a direct expression of any natural
instinct that men can be supposed to have, but that they can and do grow
up in certain social interactions. A corollary of this is that what is
beneficial is primarily the practice as a whole, not necessarily each single
act that falls under it. The third is that promising involves the *fiction* that
we create an obligation by a special act of the mind, the willing of that
very obligation. The first and second of these three claims seem to me to
be correct, but not the third.

Hume mischievously compares the fiction which he finds in
promising with the religious notions of transubstantiation and holy
orders – the idea that ordination produces some indelible though
invisible change in a man. These mysterious changes are no doubt
fictional, but they are not really comparable to the alleged fiction in
promising, for they are supposed to be brought about by divine

participation, not by anything like the logical trick of creating an obligation by saying that you are doing so. But, as Hume himself would say, the real, as opposed to the fictional, working of ordination is conventional; it is analogous to the real working of promising, and indeed involves it, since the ordinand is, among other things, undertaking new obligations, which are constituted by other people's demands and expectations, as well as by his own sentiments.

At the end of III ii 5 Hume throws in a further proof of the artificial and social origin of the obligation to keep promises. Force is held to invalidate contracts, and to free us from their obligation. But force – he must mean duress – is not significantly different from the other motives that may induce us to make a promise. A man who is dangerously wounded may promise a surgeon a large sum if he will save his life; is this so very different from promising a large sum to a kidnapper if he will let you go? So far as the promiser's own motives and actions are concerned, there is no great difference that could make the first promise valid but the second invalid. The distinction must rest on 'public interest and convenience', the fact that we want to discourage kidnappers but encourage surgeons. The argument does confirm Hume's thesis; nevertheless, its premise needs qualification. Within a legal order, promises to kidnappers and the like are regarded as invalid and unenforceable, but (as Hobbes argued) outside civil society even a promise made under duress is valid.[3] This holds for reasons which Hume himself must acknowledge. The institution of promising may be to the common advantage of kidnappers and their victims, or of conquerors and conquered – to the second party in each case because it is better to stay alive, even though impoverished or enslaved, than to be killed – but these advantages will accrue only if such promises are respected and kept.

3   THE ARTIFICIALITY OF JUSTICE   (*TREATISE* III ii 6)

Hume adds some further arguments to show that justice is an artificial, not a natural, virtue. The definition of justice as giving everyone his due presupposes that there are rights and property which constitute what is due to each person, but no relations of property and rights, taken simply as relations between the owner and his goods (or between the right-holder and what he has a right to) by themselves, and apart from our sentiments, can be found. So the basic thing must be the feeling that one should leave goods, for example, to their first possessor; the property relation depends on the virtue, not (as the above-quoted definition might suggest) the virtue on the property relation. But once we describe the virtue correctly, without the circularity implicit in the quoted definition, it is clear that we have no natural sentiment in favour of it. This becomes still plainer when we note the complexity and variability of the rules that determine property: we should need to have natural sentiments not only for leaving goods with their first possessor but also for leaving them with persons who have acquired them in a variety of arbitrarily determined ways. These complex rules (Hume now admits, rather in contrast with what he said in III ii 3) can be seen to tend to the public good; but even if this had been their primary purpose both they and the virtue of obeying them would still have been artificial, because the rules would have been *contrived* for this end; and in any case this is not their primary purpose: as he argued in III ii 2, if people had had a strong regard for the public good, the rules of justice and property would not have been needed.

Hume is right to extract or isolate the synthetic moral rules – for example, that one should leave goods with their first possessor – from the tautologous thesis that one should give everyone his due, or leave property with its owner. But, when the synthetic rule is isolated, it is not as clear as he thinks that we have no natural, instinctive, sentiment in favour of it. That we *could* have had such a natural sentiment at least with regard to the possession of goods of certain kinds is proved by the occurrence of territorial instincts in many animal species. A male robin will keep other male robins out of a certain area, and presumably he succeeds in doing so because each male fights with more energy and conviction on his home ground than when he invades another's territory. Nevertheless, Hume may be right in saying that human beings do not have such instincts, and in any case the complex and variable rules recognized in legal systems must be artificial and conventional, whether or not they can be seen as founded on some instinctive sentiments about possessions.

A second argument is that anything natural admits of gradations, with one character shading into another, whereas property rights do not. Either a man is, absolutely, the owner of an item of property or he is not. But this argument seems weak. It is not obvious that everything natural admits of gradations. A chemical element, or even a compound, must be either one thing or another. Hydrogen doesn't shade into helium, or water into hydrogen peroxide. In any case, Hume admits that moral claims to property do admit of conflicts and balances and half-rights, so the only things that this argument would prove to be artificial are the sometimes arbitrary decisions that courts of law have to give; they may have to decide a case on rather frivolous grounds, because they are constrained to decide it one way or the other. And even the civil law, Hume admits, talks of perfect and imperfect dominion; so even the law allows some gradations.

A third argument is that the use, in law and morality, of universal and inflexible rules is a proof of their artificial character. In our natural deliberations we do not constrain ourselves by universal rules, but weigh various considerations against one another. Hume thinks that if we allowed a similar weighing of various relevant and competing considerations about the allocation of property 'this wou'd produce an infinite confusion in human society ... the avidity and partiality of men wou'd quickly bring disorder into the world, if not restrain'd by some general and inflexible principles'. This is a good reason for having some inflexible rules about property (and perhaps about some other things for which people compete) and where we have such rules for this reason they are no doubt artificial. But this argument yields no proof of the artificial character of any broader and sometimes conflicting principles with regard to rights of various sorts. It says nothing about many elements in the virtues of honesty, fidelity, and the like which we should want to class as artificial on other grounds. For example, it would usually be recognized that not all promises are absolutely binding, and that some not only may but also should be broken if some sufficient reason should arise. Yet fidelity to promises in general must be classed as an artificial virtue.

4   THE ORIGIN OF GOVERNMENT AND THE LIMITS OF POLITICAL OBLIGATION   (*TREATISE* III ii 7–10)

Hume has argued that the essential basic principles of justice – the stability of possession, its transference by consent, and the performance of promises – are supported by long-range self-interest operating indirectly through conventions: each person's conformity to these laws is rationally motivated by the advantages he will receive from the conformity of others, together with his knowledge that their conformity is conditional upon his. But Hume now admits that this rational motivation may not be enough; though conformity to the rules of justice is advantageous in the long run, it may be more advantageous in the short run to violate them, and human beings have a deplorable tendency

106

to prefer smaller immediate advantages to greater remote ones. Also, if I know that you are liable to do this, I cannot rely on your conformity, even if I conform; and then it will not after all be even in my long-term interest to conform. 'I should be the cully of my integrity, if I alone shou'd impose on myself a severe restraint amidst the licentiousness of others.' Thus the reciprocally sanctioning acceptance of the rules of justice breaks down. We have come back practically to Hobbes's position after all: everyone would rationally obey the laws of nature, as a means to his own welfare, if he could trust others to do so too, but no one can trust anyone else without some further sanction.

The problem seems insoluble, because it would have to be solved by the voluntary choices of the various people involved, and the trouble lies just in their tendency to prefer smaller immediate gains to greater remote ones. If they have this tendency, how can they voluntarily set up anything to oppose it: 'if it be impossible for us to prefer what is remote, 'tis equally impossible for us to submit to any necessity, which wou'd oblige us to such a method of acting.' However, Hume discovers a neat solution. Suppose that there is something which, if I do it on December 1st, will cause me a disadvantage on December 2nd, but will bring me an advantage that more than compensates for this on December 31st. On December 1st I am liable to be swayed by the nearness of what will happen on the 2nd, as compared with the remoteness of what will happen on the 31st, and so not perform this prudent action. But eleven months earlier, on January 1st, December 2nd and December 31st are almost equally remote, so from that point of view, even given my deplorable tendency to prefer smaller immediate advantages, I shall prefer that I should perform the prudent action on December 1st. So, if there is any way in which I can, on January 1st, bind myself to do this action on December 1st, I shall adopt it. Adopting it will fit in not only with prudence but also with my actual, less than thoroughly prudent, tendencies. The device by which this pattern of motivation can take effect is government: we take steps in advance to put a few people, magistrates and rulers, in such a position that it will be in their *immediate* interest that the rules of justice should be observed, and that they will have the power to enforce them. In terms of the example, on January 1st I give the prospective magistrate something that will make him both willing and able to force me, on December, 1st to do what I now, on January 1st, prefer that I should then do, but which, left to myself, I shall not prefer on December 1st.

Just as Hume's present problem is close to Hobbes's problem, his solution is close to Hobbes's solution. But Hume does not require that the government should have absolute power, and indeed this is neither possible nor necessary. It is not possible, because the power of any ruler, however absolute in appearance, depends in reality on what his subordinate officials will do when he tells them, and ultimately on what the mass of his subjects will put up with. (Though of course he will try to arrange things so that his subordinates will find it in their interest to do what he says, and his subjects may put up with a lot for fear of worse.) It is not necessary if Hume is right in saying that the possibility of conventions and reciprocal sanctions makes it in each person's long-term interest to accept the principles of justice, so that the device of government is needed only to tip the balance against our tendency to prefer short-term advantages. To be lastingly viable, a government must make it a large part of its business to enforce the same rules that sufficient prudence would have led its subjects to observe, even left to themselves. To do this, it will not need absolute power.

Hume thus sees the primary function of rulers as being to enforce the principles of justice. But they will naturally also take on the associated task of deciding controversies about the interpretation and application of these principles, and they will be well placed to do so, since they will usually be impartial as between the litigants. But governments take on a further function also: a government may force its subjects 'to seek their own advantage, by a concurrence in some common end or purpose'. That is, it may organize co-operative efforts for long-term benefits where the direct operation of agreement and convention would fail, because of people's shortsightedness.

> Thus bridges are built; harbours open'd; ramparts rais'd; canals form'd; fleets equipp'd; and armies disciplin'd; every where, by the care of government, which, tho' composed of men subject to all human infirmities, becomes, by one of the finest and most subtle inventions imaginable, a composition, which is, in some measure, exempted from all these infirmities.

Of course, this idealized picture is not the whole truth about governments, nor, as we shall see, did Hume think it was.

In III ii 8 Hume says that small and primitive societies, where there is little conflict over possessions, can do without governments. But war, even among primitive tribes, will create the need for rulers, by putting their members into situations where their immediate selfish interests are in conflict with one another and with the joint purpose of prosecuting the war. He might have added that when the risk of sudden death increases, this strengthens our tendency to prefer immediate advantages to remote ones; in this way war accentuates the problem which may make government necessary.

Since Hume allows that there can be society without government, but not without the three fundamental rules of justice, including that of promise-keeping, he admits that it is likely that when rulers were first instituted, their subjects would have *promised* to obey them. This leads Hume to discuss the contract theory of political obligation, both in this section and in his well-known later essay, 'Of the Original Contract', which covers much the same ground. Though he grants that there was an element of contract in the setting up of the first governments, he argues that this theory is entirely erroneous with regard to governments in general, and that it is a mistake now to base political obligation ('the duty of allegiance') on contract.

Philosophers who have thought that there is a natural obligation to obey the three fundamental rules of justice, whereas political obligation is more obviously artificial, have understandably tried to base the latter on the former. But the temptation to do this is, Hume thinks, reduced when we realize that even these three rules are artificial. He concedes that the three rules together are prior to government, in that the first function of government is to enforce them; but to say this is not to base political obligation on one of the three in particular, that of promise-keeping, by way of a contract. Self-interest supports both promise-keeping and political obedience, but for different reasons. 'To obey the civil magistrate is requisite to preserve order and concord in society. To perform promises is requisite to beget mutual trust and confidence in the common offices of life.'

Hume also argues that promises have force especially where a secure guarantee of action is needed, and other motives are not sufficient to ensure this. But the general motives for political obedience are so strong that the support of promises is not needed here. 'Our civil duties, therefore, must soon detach themselves from our promises, and acquire a separate force and influence.' There is no more reason to base allegiance on a supposed promise than to base honesty, the abstaining from the possessions of others, on this; each of these is supported independently by considerations of interest. Allegiance also has an independent moral sentiment in its favour, as well as an interested motive, because we can see the good it does to society in general and the harm caused by disloyalty and sedition – particularly when it is others, not ourselves, who engage in them. Our moral condemnation of rebellion, because of the harm it does, is separate from our moral condemnation of promise-breaking, which is due to our awareness of the different sort of harm it produces.

Hume thinks that the contract theory of political obligation is directly falsified by the way in which both governments and subjects treat the duty of allegiance and the crime of treason. People are thought of as owing obedience to the government of the country in which they grow up even when they have had no opportunity to contract into this society or to opt out of it, even if a government forbids its subjects to emigrate, and even if it is absolute in other ways, not making its acts conditional upon the consent of the governed. If present-day allegiance rested on a promise, even a tacit one, people generally could not fail to know this. Since most of them do not believe this, the contract theory cannot be correct. In Hume's time, this was a forceful addition to his other arguments; somewhat ironically, it has since become less cogent, in that at least a vague form of the view that government derives its legitimacy from the consent of the governed is now widely held, and even tyrannical rulers try to maintain the fiction that they are supported by some kind of popular will. But Hume's other arguments, that there are in general reasons of self-interest for accepting an existing government and reasons based on the general happiness for approving of such loyalty and condemning sedition, quite independent of any alleged contracts or promises, remain in force.

Hume's theory has obvious implications, which he draws in III ii 9, with regard to the limits of political obligation. There is no need to base the right to resist tyrannical rulers on a supposed contract; this right follows directly from the reasons we ordinarily have for obedience. Rulers are human, and subject to all the ordinary human temptations and vices; not surprisingly, some of them become tyrants and public enemies. If an established government rules very badly, and no longer gives its subjects the security and protection that are its *raison d'être*, it will be in their interest to rebel and try to change it, provided that the chance of getting a better government is sufficiently good to outweigh the harm that is certain to be done by the convulsions which always attend revolutions. Rebellion will also meet with moral approval under the same condition. And that is all there is to be said about it. Hume is confident that common sense will lead people to these conclusions, even if they do not clearly understand the political theory which entails them. He stresses, however, in III ii 10, that

110

We ought always to weigh the advantages, which we reap from authority, against the disadvantages; and by this means we shall become more scrupulous of putting in practice the doctrine of resistance. The common rule requires submission; and 'tis only in cases of grievous tyranny and oppression, that the exception can take place.

The section (III ii 10) which deals with 'the objects of allegiance' – that is, the particular men or bodies of men to whom we owe political obedience – is remarkable mainly for what it does not say. There is no more than a hint of the democratic assumption that a legitimate authority must be one that is chosen or preferred by the majority of the members of the community in question. This is, Hume agrees, the initial situation when a government is first set up; but it does not last. Once a government has been in existence for any length of time, 'We naturally suppose ourselves born to submission.' As he has argued, the real motive for submission is self-interest; but this does not determine who the rulers are to be. About that different subjects would have divergent interests, so to let the choice of rulers depend on those interests would produce endless confusion. Nor would it be any better if we tried to choose as rulers those who would serve the public interest best: though there is a unitary public interest, there are wildly conflicting opinions about it, so that this principle, too, would generate confusion. The reasons of self-interest which we have for accepting government in general are also reasons for not being too particular about what government we have. If we are too eager for perfection, we shall only perpetuate confusion – as, Hume thinks, we would if we aimed at the best possible distribution of property. In order to resolve conflicts over possessions we have to accept and follow rather arbitrary principles for the assignment of goods to persons, which are determined largely by the imagination and which often issue in allocations that are in themselves absurd and deplorable; similarly, in order to get stable governments we have to proceed by general rules, again based largely on the imagination, even though they often result in men becoming rulers whom no one would dream of choosing on their merits.

These imagination-based principles are as follows. (i) Long possession, by any one form of government or royal family. (ii) Present possession. (iii) Conquest. (iv) Hereditary succession: a son is accepted as his father's successor, and Hume notes that this principle tends to intrude even into elective monarchies. (v) Positive laws: Hume is thinking here of a case where a legislature, itself in power for one or more of the above-listed reasons, tried explicitly to introduce a new form of government. He notes that a new government thus set up will tend not to acquire at once all the authority of whatever pre-existing body created it; its subjects will have some tendency to revert to the old, long-established, constitution.

Hume is here simply describing the bases of the authority of the mainly monarchical governments in Europe in his time, while taking a cynical view of arguments about their legitimacy. Anyone who studies history and sees to how great an extent present royal power goes back to successful usurpation and conquest

> will soon learn to treat very lightly all disputes concerning the rights of princes, and will be convinc'd, that a strict adherence to any general rules, and the rigid loyalty to particular persons and families, on which some people set so high a value, are virtues that hold less of reason, than of bigotry and superstition.

Here, of course, he is arguing against the Jacobites and in favour of the House of Hanover; he also points out that the revolution of 1688 was the easier to carry through and the easier to approve of because the previously established constitution was a mixed one, not a pure monarchy. But he is not keen to discuss the merits of that revolution; rather he uses it to illustrate the thesis to which he constantly returns about the influence of the imagination. Because James II was deposed as a bad ruler, association with him made it easy to exclude his infant son from the succession, whereas if James II had died before he was deposed, people would have felt that his son had the right to succeed. He concludes with the paradox that kings often seem to derive a right from their successors, as well as from their ancestors. The stable reigns of Anne, George I, and George II make William III look legitimate, and 'The present *king* of *France* makes *Hugh Capet* a more lawful prince than *Cromwell*', merely because of these two usurpers, Hugh Capet had the good fortune, as Oliver Cromwell did not, to become the ancestor of a long line of kings.

Hume's cynicism about the legitimacy of royal authority is certainly justified. He considers the argument that utility itself justifies the hereditary principle, because this is the best way of avoiding the anarchy and confusion that would result from trying to elect our rulers. But he replies that utility entails only that succession to the crown should be fixed somehow or other, and that some further (imaginative) influence must be at work to determine the hereditary principle and to get it accepted in so many countries throughout the world. The controversial question is the one which, as I said, he dismisses almost without consideration, whether there is a viable democratic method of choosing both the form of government and its personnel. What we can say is that if he is right, as he seems to be, about the basic reason for having governments, there can be no universally applicable principle to the effect that only democratically chosen governments are legitimate, and what kind of government will actually work, or work best, will depend on the particular circumstances of the country in question. To say what this implies in any detail would take us too far away from Hume's text.

5 INTERNATIONAL JUSTICE (*TREATISE* III ii 11)

Once governments are established in a number of different but adjacent countries, each state operates as a unit in relation to the other states. They are thus quasi-individuals, and the same forces that have produced the artificial virtues that are the elements of justice between individuals will similarly produce rules to control the interactions between states. But although states, in relation to one another, are in some ways like ordinary individuals, they are also very different in other ways, so that what we get here is a new set of rules, the 'laws of nations' or international law. Hume lists such things as the sacredness of the persons of ambassadors, the declaration of war, and the abstaining from poisoned arms. However, these special rules must be seen as being superadded to the ordinary rules of justice: the stability of possession, its transference by consent, and the performance of promises are, he says, duties of princes as well as of subjects, and for the same reasons of interest. Where possession is not stable, there will be perpetual war. Where property is not transferred by consent, there can be no trade. Where promises are not kept, there can be no leagues and alliances. So the benefits of peace, trade, and mutual assistance provide motives for the observance of these rules by states in relation to one another, just as they give individuals reasons for observing them.

On the other hand Hume notes that 'There is a maxim very current in the world, which few politicians are willing to avow, but which has been authoriz'd by the practice of all ages, *that there is a system of morals calculated for princes, much more free than that which ought to govern private persons.*' Princes do make treaties with one another, and each expects the other to keep the agreement: no one will say that the most solemn treaties ought to have *no* force. Yet it is generally accepted, in the actual practice of statesmen, that these agreements have less force than promises between individuals, and may be broken on slighter excuses.

This initially shocking proposition can, Hume says, be explained on his principles: 'tho' the intercourse of different states be advantageous, and even sometimes necessary, yet it is not so necessary nor advantageous as that among individuals, without which 'tis utterly impossible for human nature ever to subsist.' In other words, it is not so important that states should keep peace with one another, trade, and co-operate in other ways as that neighbouring individuals should do so. There is a stronger self-interest in favour of justice between individuals than in favour of justice between states. Hume thinks that the moral sentiment in favour of justice between individuals is derived from benevolence, along with our understanding of the benefits that result for everyone from the system of obedience to the rules of justice. It follows that, since conflicts and non-co-operation between states − the natural result of failures to maintain justice − do less harm to people in general than conflicts and non-co-operation between individuals, the moral sentiment in favour of just dealings between states will also be weaker.

We cannot, Hume thinks, say *how much* weaker; but he believes that those who practise politics will develop a feel for this; they will gradually learn how scrupulous they need, or need not, be in their international transactions. He uses this as a proof that people implicitly recognize the conventional status of the rules of justice. Only on the assumption that these rules arise from interest by way of conventions can we understand how their moral stringency diminishes when they are transferred to a sphere where the relevant interests are less strong; so he concludes that those who (in practice) admit their diminished stringency as between states have an implicit understanding that they arise merely from conventions and from the interest we have in preserving peace, order, and co-operation.

In commenting previously on this passage I have remarked that while Hume may have been right about the smaller amount of harm done by wars between states, in his time, than would be done by a breakdown of justice between individuals, the position is now reversed: the risk of world war is an immediate threat to the very survival of the human race.[4] But even in the circumstances of his own time Hume's account is open to criticism.

The main reason why statesmen feel less bound to be honest in their international dealings than in interpersonal dealings is not, surely, that international peace and co-operation matter less than interpersonal peace and co-operation (whether this holds, or held, or not) but simply that they have not yet been so securely established. As Hobbes pointed out, sovereign states are constantly in what he called a state of war with one another: they are not fighting all the time, but they are always on the brink of doing so, and are armed and prepared for war. It is significant that the special 'laws of nations' which Hume mentions plainly presuppose this state of war; they have the function only of mitigating conflicts and making it easier to maintain intervals of non-fighting within a lasting state of war, not that of establishing justice and genuine peace between nations. As Hobbes said also, 'the laws of nature oblige *in foro interno* ... to a desire they should take place: but *in foro externo* ... to the putting them in act, not always.' Because there is not yet – and certainly was not in Hume's time – a stable international system of justice, no one state can afford to obey the rules of justice thoroughly and undeviatingly; if it did, it would become 'the cully of its own integrity'. The conventions and reciprocal sanctions we examined in (i) above do not yet operate securely between sovereign states. (But it would not be true to say that they do not work at all: nuclear war has been staved off since 1949 by the balance of terror.)

The point is not, as is sometimes thought, that statesmen sacrifice international morality to national interest or to their special duty towards those whom they govern and represent. Of course each state, acting as a unit through those who represent it, will in the main pursue what seems to be its interest. But so do individuals in their interpersonal dealings. What is important is that whereas, if Hume is right, self-interest in individuals makes them on the whole accept and support the rules of interpersonal justice, the self-interest of states has only a much weaker tendency to make them accept and support any rules of international justice. And the reason is not that international justice matters less, but that as yet there is much less of an established system of justice between states. However, in thus correcting Hume's account of why international morality is regarded as less stringent than interpersonal morality, we do not undermine but rather strengthen his argument that this state of affairs reveals some implicit understanding of the conventional basis of morality, for it is precisely the conventional structure that is weaker in the international field.

But, further, international justice is a test case for Hume's thesis that self-interest alone, by way of conventions, could establish a system of justice if people were prudent enough, if only they did not discount, in some proportion, remoter advantages and disadvantages. For in international dealings we have the requisite self-interest and the clear possibility of friendly or hostile reciprocation, in varying degrees and with plain indications. Perhaps the trouble is that a sovereign state is a pretty inadequate sort of individual, rendered incapable of taking and acting on long-range views by the way in which it is organized to act as a unit, the way in which its government is set up and changed: electors as such do not look far ahead, and politicians cannot look further than the next election. On this view, a state is by nature analogous to those individuals in whom mental defect produces diminished responsibility. But it is disputable whether this holds for an organized government as a whole, even in a democracy. The weakness of the international system suggests that some other vital factor, present in the interpersonal case, is lacking here. Hobbes, of course, would take this as a confirmation of his thesis that a sovereign is needed. Plainly, we do not have an international sovereign; such an organization as the United Nations falls far short of this status, as did the League of Nations before it. But, alternatively, we could take this is an illustration of a point made earlier, that the full case for justice based on self-interest rests partly on the assumption that people's actions are governed by relatively stable dispositions, and partly also on the fact that they have moral feelings which help to control their actions. Indirectly, the moral sentiment in favour of justice helps to commend the practice of it to self-interest. The moral sentiments are clearly weaker in the international case, and so weaken the structure of conventions and reciprocal sanctions. And there is a vicious spiral here: for reasons already stated, the weakening of this structure will in turn weaken the moral sentiments. But if the trouble lies in this weakness of international moral sentiments, or in a lack of reliably stable dispositions or, again, in an inability of states to act on sufficiently long-range views of their self-interest, then some strengthening of international government might be a remedy, even if the Hobbesian demand for a sovereign is mistaken. Government, after all, is Hume's own remedy for individual shortsightedness.

This suggests a partial revision of Hume's account of justice. He has argued that (given enough prudence) self-interest will generate conventions and establish the practice of justice; that realization of its good effect on the well-being of a community, conjoined with natural benevolence, leads to a moral approval of justice; that government comes in to compensate for shortsightedness, for insufficient prudence; and that international justice is weaker only because it is less needed. I suggest rather that the different elements work together to a much greater extent. The full prudential case for the practice of justice presupposes not only fairly stable dispositions but also moral sentiments and a reserve of legal sanctions, while legal sanctions in turn need a backing in moral sentiment as well as the power of a government to enforce them. Without the moral, legal, and governmental development there can be only a fragile basic system of conventions with reciprocal sanctioning, always liable to be wrecked by shortsighted actions. In the interpersonal case we can see this as the foundation on which a much more elaborate and secure system has been built, with moral sentiments (especially about the rights of others) fixing boundaries within which people pursue their own interests; but in the international case there is little more than the basic system.

This leads to a further comment on Hume's description of international morality. He hesitates between saying that it contains the same rules as interpersonal justice, but they are less strictly observed and are felt to be less binding, and saying that it contains different rules. These would be not only the special laws of nations about ambassadors, not engaging in undeclared war, and the like, but also, for example, a variety of agreement that is understood to be weaker, one with an implied clause 'provided that keeping this treaty does not become too harmful to our foreseeable national interest'. We might refer here also to the practice of making agreements that run for a limited number of years, and will then lapse or be re-negotiated in the light of changed conditions. Such an intrinsically weaker sytem of rules could still be fairly well respected, and perhaps this is what Hume meant when he spoke about the practice of the world teaching us the degrees of our duty. If this second view of the matter is correct, there already is a system of international morality, though a thin one. Sovereign states are not in Hobbes's state of war, but in a condition intermediate between this and a full system of justice. There are rules, more or less recognized and respected, which, while they do not establish peace in a full sense, have some tendency to restrict conflict. This falls far short of the standard of interpersonal justice as it exists within any even moderately decent state, though this in turn falls far short of the ideal of total co-operation put forward by utilitarian and Christian moralists. But it may well be that this thin international system is inadequate even to limit the harm done by conflicts between states, in view of the technical resources available for modern wars.

In any case, the problem of international justice and security is not, as

Hume thought, only a minor extension of the general theory of justice. It is at once a test case for the rival theories in this field and a practical problem which, because it is so pressing, makes it all the more important that we should get the theory right.

6 CHASTITY AND MODESTY (*TREATISE* III ii 12)

Hume's explanation of the traditional moral rules that demand chastity and modesty in women uses very familiar points − used also, for example, by Hutcheson − but in an unusual way. He takes it to be obvious that these are not natural virtues: there are no instinctive tendencies in favour of chastity or modesty, and equally no instinctive tendency to approve of them or to disapprove of their opposites. So again we must trace them to 'voluntary conventions' and 'the interest of society'.

Both men and women, he assumes, have a natural concern for their own offspring. The long duration of human infancy, the period throughout which children need care and protection, therefore makes necessary lasting unions between men and women. But men will not put up with this restraint, and with the trouble of providing for children, unless they have an assurance that the children in question are their own, and only chastity in their wives will give them this assurance. Such chastity could not be guaranteed by legal rules and penalties alone, but only by a very strong moral pressure. Even a strong moral pressure in favour of chastity would not do the trick; if women were exposed to sexual temptation they would be sure to yield to it, despite the moral pressure. What is needed, therefore, is a further moral pressure in favour of such a degree of modesty in dress, behaviour, and so on, as will ensure that women are not even tempted to be unchaste.

Hume suggests that a speculative philosopher might reason *a priori* on these lines, and conclude that we *need* strong moral sentiments supporting such modesty as well as chastity in women, and yet he might despair of the possibility of actually creating them. He means, I think, that nothing like Mandeville's flattery and panegyrics and statues could have so dramatic an effect. 'But', he says,

> speculative reasonings, which cost so much pains to philosophers, are often form'd by the world naturally, and without reflection. ... Those, who have an interest in the fidelity of women, naturally disapprove of

their infidelity, and all the approaches to it. Those, who have no
interest, are carried along with the stream. Education takes possession
of the ductile minds of the fair sex in their infancy. ....

But this is far too facile. The machinery he suggests here for producing
these sentiments is quite inadequate. Each husband has, no doubt, an
interest in his own wife's fidelity; but he may have no interest in the
fidelity or modesty of other men's wives, but rather the reverse; and the
same applies to unmarried women. One would expect that the majority
influence would be against chastity and modesty, and that if the fair sex
had such ductile minds as Hume (in his twenties) supposed, they would
have been led in an opposite direction. A further difficulty is that the
degree of modesty to which his argument points is rather that which has
been traditional in Islamic society than that which was normal in
Europe even in the eighteenth century.

Yet presumably there is some process by which the world has created
these sentiments naturally and without reflection, and indeed at least the
outline of a better explanation could be constructed with Hume's
materials. First, if wives are seen as being in some ways analogous to
property – for example, as a potential source of conflict – then the same
sorts of consideration that produce the rules of honesty with regard to
property and that support both the practice of these rules and moral
approval of them will generate rules which condemn adultery, but
condemn both the men and the women who engage in it. But, secondly,
since the harm done by adultery is seen as affecting more directly the
situation in which the woman is involved, the pressure against it will be
directed more towards her than towards the man. Thirdly, in a male
dominated society, women, in their own interest, must aim at being
wanted as wives and at continuing to be so wanted, and for the reasons
Hume gives chastity and modesty will help significantly towards this –
but perhaps not modesty in an Islamic degree. Something like this would
be the basic explanation, though no doubt there are many epicycles in
the theory needed to explain sexual morality as a whole, including the
considerable variations found in different societies and at different times.
And some of the elements are ambiguous: as Anatole France says about
the introduction of clothes, in *Penguin Island*, 'It is certain that modesty
communicates an invincible attraction to women.'

VII

THE NATURAL VIRTUES

(*TREATISE* III iii 1–5)

Hume turns in III iii 1 to the natural virtues. He insists, as before, that 'moral distinctions depend entirely on certain peculiar sentiments of pain and pleasure ... whatever mental quality in ourselves or others gives us a satisfaction, by the survey or reflexion, is of course virtuous; as every thing of this nature, that gives uneasiness, is vicious.' A virtue, then, will be any mental quality which, if we detect it in others, tends to produce love for them, and if we detect it in ourselves, tends to produce pride. In order to explain why the qualities in question do tend to produce love and pride he relies on the assumption that 'sympathy is a very powerful principle in human nature.' He shows how powerful it is by using it to explain at least part of our sense of beauty: we find beautiful those things that, being useful, tend to produce pleasure in those who possess them, and thus to find them beautiful is to share, by sympathy, the possessor's pleasure. Also, Hume argues, it is only through sympathy that we approve of the artificial virtues, by seeing them as good for society and by sharing, through sympathy, the happiness of people in general which they promote. It is then easy to use this same principle of sympathy to explain our approval of the natural virtues, which also tend to the good of mankind.

Variations in the meaning of the word 'sympathy' may obscure Hume's line of thought here. 'Sympathy' does not (as it often does in modern use) mean 'compassion' or 'pity', but rather a tendency to share what one takes to be the feelings of another, of whatever kind they are; sympathy is *Mitgefühl*, not *Mitleid*. Nor is it another word for benevolence or for altruism; but sympathy can and normally will produce benevolence. In so far as I share someone else's feelings, his happiness and his misery will matter to me; I shall desire his happiness in the same way that I desire my own, though no doubt in a lower degree. Thus Hume does not, like Hutcheson or Shaftesbury or Butler, take benevolence as a basic given element in human nature, but explains it as resulting from sympathy. He has also offered (in II i 11) an explanation of sympathy itself: we have always a lively idea or impression of ourselves, this communicates liveliness to any idea associated (for example by resemblance) with it, so the idea that we have of the feelings of beings who resemble us is so enlivened as to be 'converted into an impression'. In the *Enquiry*, however, Hume abandons these explanatory psychological theories, and falls back on the mere fact of benevolence: 'It is needless to push our researches so far as to ask, why we have humanity or a fellow-feeling with others. It is sufficient, that this is experienced to be a principle in human nature.'[1]

Among the natural virtues Hume lists 'Meekness, beneficence, charity, generosity, clemency, moderation, equity', and he thinks it is even easier to explain our approval of them by sympathy than our approval of the artificial virtues, because the exercise of any of these natural virtues obviously and directly benefits the persons towards whom they are exercised, whereas, as we have seen, particular acts of justice may not be beneficial to those most affected or even to society as a whole; it is only the complete system of justice and property that is beneficial.

However, the explanation of our recognition of the natural virtues as virtues, that is, our approval of these specific qualities, is not quite as simple as it might seem. One difficulty is that many things which produce variations in the degree of sympathy do not produce similar variations in moral approval. We sympathize more with people who are in one way or another nearer to us than with strangers, foreigners, and those remote in time or place, but we set the same moral evaluation on similar characters and actions wherever they are found. Hume tries to resolve this difficulty: ' 'tis impossible we cou'd ever converse together on any reasonable terms, were each of us to consider characters and persons, only as they appear from his peculiar point of view. In order ... to prevent these continual *contradictions*, and arrive at a more *stable* judgment of things, we fix on some *steady* and *general* points of view', and he speaks of 'correcting our sentiments, or at least, of correcting our language'. He says

We blame equally a bad action, which we read of in history, with one perform'd in our neighbourhood t'other day: The meaning of which is, that we know from reflexion, that the former action wou'd excite as strong sentiments of disapprobation as the latter, were it plac'd in the same position.

Hume is here coming down in favour of one rather than another of the views that I contrasted (in chapter V) as variants of sentimentalism. A moral judgment, he is here saying, neither reports nor expresses the speaker's actual sentiments, but says what sentiments the speaker would have if the action which he is judging affected persons close to him. Or, since he has said that we want to converse together using moral terms without confusion, perhaps he does or should mean that the judgment says what sentiments any ordinary person would feel if the action affected persons close to him. But it is not at all plausible to say that this is what a typical moral judgment *means*, that this is what a standard speaker intends to convey when he makes such a judgment and is given, by the language, a conventional means of conveying. Even if it were, we might ask why we should be so keen to make judgments that had such a meaning. It was misleading of Hume to suggest that uncorrected judgments, directly expressive of sympathy and therefore correlated with the actual degrees of sympathy, would involve continual contradictions. If moral judgments were understood to be immediately expressive of sympathy, their differences would not be felt as contradictions. The truth is that moral judgments, even about what Hume classes as natural virtues, belong to a system of evaluation which tends to be, and is intended by those who engage in it to be, both interpersonal and impartial: it is expected that different speakers will judge similarly about intrinsically similar actions, no matter how differently those actions or their agents may be related to them. That being so, it is very natural for those who think and speak within this system to take the further step of objectifying their evaluations, to think and feel that in calling an action virtuous or vicious they are simply describing it as it is in itself, that to find the virtue or the vice they do not, after all, have to turn their reflection into their own breasts, or into the breasts of any other people. But whether they take this further step or not, we can ask why there should be this drive towards an interpersonal and impartial system of evaluation. This is not immediately explained by what Hume admits to be the extremely variable operations of sympathy. But the answer is not hard to find. We have this system because it is, in more than one way, useful to have it. This uniform system of evaluation serves as a steady encouragement of the dispositions that count as natural virtues and as a steady discouragement of the contrary vices. To approve of a certain disposition is to be pleased with it, and this pleasure, either in the person who has the disposition or in others of whose feelings he is aware, and whose feelings he tends therefore to share through sympathy, will reward and reinforce that disposition, and disapproval will work in a corresponding but opposite way. Also, in so far as moral evaluations are, in appropriate circumstances, prescriptive or action-guiding, this system of evaluations will tend to control conduct directly, not only by way of these dispositions. The natural virtues are most immediately beneficial to those directly related to their exercise, but even in this restricted area they are most likely to have their full effect if they are valued interpersonally and impartially. But, as Hume says, they also have a tendency to the good of society. They, too, like the artificial virtues, counteract those effects of selfishness and merely confined generosity – self-referential altruism – which, by fostering conflicts, tend to make things worse for everyone. The natural virtues, as supported by a 'steady and general' approval of them, are an additional element in the 'more elaborate and secure system' of which I spoke near the end of chapter VI, section 4.

Obvious though this answer is, it is rather devastating for Hume's theory. For it means that his natural virtues are, after all, a further set of artificial virtues. Although we may have some instinctive tendencies to develop these dispositions and to act in these ways, and also to react favourably to some instances of these dispositions and actions (namely those that are close to us), the precise way in which we approve of them (namely interpersonally and impartially) must, like the rules of justice, be understood as a system which flourishes because *as a system* it serves a social function, helping human beings who are made pretty competitive both by their genetic make-up and by their situation to live together fairly peacefully and with a certain amount of mutual aid and co-operation. Though the psychology of sympathy may play some part, the natural virtues themselves and the fully developed form of the recognition of them as virtues will owe a good deal to conventions and reciprocal pressures. Whereas Hume offers a sociological explanation of the artificial virtues but a psychological explanation of the natural virtues, it is now clear that an at least partly sociological explanation is needed for the natural virtues too.

This conclusion is strengthened by the second difficulty which Hume mentions. If someone has a character which would in ordinary circumstances benefit others, 'we esteem him virtuous ... even tho' particular accidents prevent its operation, and incapacitate him from being serviceable to his friends and country.' 'Virtue in rags', he says, 'is still virtue', though it doesn't actually do any good. As Kant says, the good will shines like a jewel by its own light, even if a stepmotherly nature prevents it from achieving any good results.[2] But how could sympathy alone explain such a judgment? The virtuous disposition, or good will, stripped of practical abilities and opportunities, has no tendency to promote any happiness in which sympathy could make us share. Hume's answer is no more than a restatement of the problem:

> where any object, in all its parts, is fitted to attain any agreeable end, it naturally gives us pleasure, and is esteem'd beautiful, even tho' some external circumstances be wanting to render it altogether effectual. 'Tis sufficient if every thing be compleat in the object itself.

As usual, he ascribes this to the imagination and to the way in which it 'passes easily from the cause to the effect' – that is, to what would normally be its effect. But it is more explanatory to see this as an outcome of a *system* of evaluation, which to be effective needs to be systematic, and an associated tendency to objectification. This system encourages kindly, fair, and forgiving behaviour by applying a favourable characterization to the corresponding dispositions. If it is to work in this way, those dispositions must be regularly so characterized wherever they occur, with or without the accompaniments that would make them useful. Equally, if such evaluations are to be objectified, they must be tied to the intrinsic features of the subjects to which they are applied, upon which features the supposed moral qualities can be seen as consequential or supervenient.

A third difficulty for Hume's account lies, as he says, in a contradiction 'which may appear to be betwixt the *extensive sympathy*, on which our sentiments of virtue depend, and that *limited generosity* which I have frequently observ'd to be natural to men, and which justice and property suppose'. Once more he appeals to the imagination. We have enough extensive sympathy to arouse the imagination to make a moral judgment, which is in this respect like an aesthetic judgment, though not enough directly to make us act for the benefit of someone remote from us. But this reply is awkward, since, as Hume has argued all along, moral judgments are not inert, but are meant to, and do, influence passions and actions, and do so far more strongly than aesthetic judgments. It might seem that if judgments which express extensive sympathy are able to do this, our generosity cannot be so limited after all. The solution of this paradox lies in what I said in resolving our first difficulty, that we must apply to the natural virtues also the analysis that Hume has proposed for the artificial ones. A system of interpersonal and impartial approval of humanity, generosity, compassion, clemency, fairness, and the like, where both these dispositions and the approval of them go beyond anything that is supported by instinctive sympathy or immediate benevolence, is advantageous to most people most of the time; it is a useful check on the very limited character of their instinctive altruism, and is encouraged by conventions based ultimately on self-interest (or only limited generosity) of the same kind as those which encourage what Hume has classed as artificial virtues.

Hume's summing up is that 'Every quality of the mind is denominated virtuous, which gives pleasure by the mere survey; as every quality, which produces pain, is call'd vicious', and that 'This pleasure and this pain may arise from different sources. For we reap a pleasure from the view of a character, which is naturally fitted to be useful to others, or to the person himself, or which is agreeable to others, or to the person himself.' But in all cases we choose 'some common point of view'; that is how we are able to reach agreement in our moral judgments and sentiments, and our ability to do this rests ultimately on a natural principle of sympathy. We need not deny that sympathy plays some part here; but I have argued that it cannot, by itself, provide a sufficient explanation either of our taking this common point of view or of the practical force of the moral system that we then adopt.

In III iii 2, 3, and 4 Hume sets out to confirm this general theory by showing how it will explain some of our more specific moral judgments. In fact his attention is distributed among various 'virtues' in a rather curious way. III iii 2 deals with 'greatness of mind'. Hume argues that although we disapprove of 'an overweening conceit of our own merit', and also of open, direct expressions of even a justifiably good opinion of ourselves, we approve of 'a genuine and hearty pride, or self-esteem, if well conceal'd and well founded'; 'the world naturally esteems a well-regulated pride, which secretly animates our conduct, without breaking out into such indecent expressions of vanity, as may offend the vanity of others.' The admiration paid to heroism and military courage and enterprise, even where their effects are disastrous, is one example of this tendency. The merit of self-esteem is explained by its being both useful and agreeable to its possessor, while the demerit of public expressions of self-esteem is explained by their being disagreeable to others. Hume admits that this last point belongs rather with his account of the artificial virtues. We all have a wonderful partiality for ourselves, and if we all expressed this, 'we shou'd mutually cause the greatest indignation in each other'.

> In like manner, therefore, as we establish the *laws of nature*, in order to secure property in society, and prevent the opposition of self-interest; we establish the *rules of good-breeding*, in order to prevent the opposition of men's pride, and render conversation agreeable and inoffensive.

And plainly a similar account can be given of other principles of social behaviour and the rules of etiquette; good manners are minor artificial virtues.

Hume deals in III iii 3 with goodness and benevolence. But he has little to say about them, and what he does say hardly calls for comment. These dispositions are plainly beneficial to those directly affected by them, they are qualities both immediately agreeable and useful to others, and they are both the most obvious examples of natural virtues and the ones most easily explained by Hume's principle of sympathy. The one curious point is that Hume confines his discussion to the limited, self-referential, altruism which, he thinks, is all that we can reasonably expect of people. 'When the natural tendency of his passions leads him to be serviceable and useful within his sphere, we approve of his character, and love his person, by a sympathy with the sentiments of those, who have a more particular connexion with him.' And again,

> We consider him with all his relations in society; and love or hate him, according as he affects those, who have any immediate intercourse with him. And 'tis a most certain rule, that if there be no relation of life, in which I cou'd not wish to stand to a particular person, his character must so far be allow'd to be perfect. If he be as little wanting to himself as to others, his character is entirely perfect. This is the ultimate test of merit and virtue.

It would seem that for Hume charity begins and ends pretty close to home.

It is worth noting that Mill, in a similar passage, adds a qualification which Hume fails to make explicit:[3]

the thoughts of the most virtuous man need not ... travel beyond the particular persons concerned, except so far as is necessary to assure himself that in benefiting them he is not violating the rights, that is, the legitimate and authorised expectations, of any one else.

Hume, on the other hand, suggests that all that is needed is the qualities that make someone 'a safe companion, an easy friend, a gentle master, an agreeable husband, or an indulgent father'. It may be reflected that Hume's compatriot and near-contemporary, Rob Roy, was, by Scott's well-informed account, all of these, though also a blackmailer (in the old sense of one who runs a protection racket), a bandit, and a robber.

We can, however, agree with Hume that these varieties of self-regard and self-referential altruism are virtues, and his emphasis on them is a welcome corrective to the tendency, in both Christian and utilitarian morality, to set up a quite impracticable ideal of universal benevolence. Yet it remains true that what we morally approve of and regard as virtues in this area involve a wider concern for others than either instinctive affection or immediate social intercourse would produce. Humanity, generosity, compassion, clemency, fairness, and the like must therefore be counted as partly artificial virtues with respect to their approved range of application, and not only with regard to the systematic, interpersonal, impartial, and objectifying way in which we approve of them.

In III iii 4 Hume discusses natural abilities. He means such things as intelligence, good sense, judgment, wit, and eloquence. Since these are clearly mental qualities that are either useful or agreeable either to their possessor or to others, they fall within the scope of Hume's account of what we recognize as virtues. Yet we commonly distinguish virtues from natural abilities. So this is another difficulty for his theory, which he tries to resolve in several different ways. One move he makes is to suggest that it is a merely 'grammatical' question just where we draw the line between virtues and other qualities. Since, however, he has set out to explain the phenomenon of morality, and therefore to explain why we approve and disapprove as we do, why we count just such and such dispositions as virtues and vices, he could set this difficulty aside as merely a question for grammarians only if he could first show that the difference is a purely verbal one, that so far as thought and feeling and action are concerned we treat natural abilities in the same way as what are explicitly called virtues, that it is only the name that is arbitrarily or accidentally withheld. But this is not so. While we admire judgment, say, or eloquence, we do not exactly blame someone who is deficient in them, as we do blame someone who is deficient in courage, or who falls below normal standards of honesty or kindness.

Hume considers the suggestion that there is a real difference, reflected in these differences of treatment, between natural abilities which are involuntary and moral virtues which are voluntary. But he has already (in II iii 1–2) rejected the extreme free-will doctrine; he regards all the qualities we have as being equally the result of antecedent causes, and he argues that many qualities that have been traditionally classed as virtues, such as constancy, fortitude, magnanimity, and prudence, are as involuntary as the natural abilities. He admits that 'legislators, and divines, and moralists' have been particularly concerned to regulate voluntary actions, and have concentrated on those qualities which they thought might be altered by exhortation or punishment. But he thinks that men ordinarily praise or blame whatever pleases or displeases them without regard to these possibilities of regulation.

In Appendix IV to the *Enquiry*, Hume replies to this same objection by pointing out how widely the equivalents of the term 'virtue' were used by such ancient writers as Aristotle, Caesar, Plutarch, Livy, and Polybius and by the Italian historian Guicciardini, and he develops the suggestion that the influence of theology has distorted modern philosophy:

> reasoning, and even language, have been warped from their natural course, and distinctions have been endeavoured to be established where the difference of the objects was, in a manner, imperceptible. Philosophers, or rather divines under that disguise, treating all morals as on a like footing with civil laws, guarded by the sanctions of reward and punishment, were necessarily led to render this circumstance, of *voluntary* or *involuntary*, the foundation of their whole theory.

However, the distinction between voluntary and involuntary would be important within the sociological explanation of the virtues we have found in Hume's own work; both it and the related distinction between intentional and unintentional can be drawn without assuming that there is contra-causal free will; they are as relevant to morals as to law if morality has at all the function of controlling human action and behaviour; and the classic discussion of this topic is not in any divine but in Aristotle's *Nicomachean Ethics* (Book III, chapters 1–5). If Hume is genuinely to account for the actual phenomenon of morality, he cannot ignore this distinction or any differences that rest upon it.

Another distinction is that between qualities which benefit solely or mainly their possessor and those which benefit others; but this would not mark off natural abilities from virtues. Abilities are often used mainly for the advantage of others, while many virtues, like prudence, industry, and determination are primarily of benefit to their possessors.

However, Hume has got himself into an unnecessary difficulty here. Virtues are, as Aristotle said, dispositions for choice. Abilities and dispositions for choice are in different categories, and it is in no way surprising if we have special sentiments with regard to those dispositions for choice which we have one reason or another for cultivating and reinforcing or, on the contrary, for discouraging, different from the feelings we have about natural abilities, or the lack of them, that are, in their own rather different way, pleasing or useful, or the reverse, but which are not similarly responsive to social pressure or cultivation.

Altogether, Hume's treatment of the natural virtues is both less interesting and less defensible than his treatment of the artificial ones. One great improvement would be a partial breaking down of the distinction between the two groups, so that at least in their more extensive application such virtues as humanity, generosity, compassion, clemency, and fairness were seen to be artificial in the same sense as honesty or fidelity to agreements, and to be similarly supported by what we can understand as conventions. Also, whereas Hume himself was inclined to break down the distinction between the two groups to the extent of saying that our approval of even the artificial ones is natural, since it proceeds from our sympathy with the interests of society, conjoined with our realization that justice tends to the public good, I think that this distinction should be broken down in the opposite way: our interpersonal, impartial, objectifying approval of the natural virtues, no less than of the artificial ones, should be understood as a system of evaluation which has much the same social function as the artificial virtues themselves.

VIII

SOME SUCCESSORS: SMITH, PRICE, REID

Adam Smith is fully in agreement with Hume in regarding morality as a matter of sentiment – so much so that he bluntly entitles his work *The Theory of Moral Sentiments*. He also agrees with Hume in tracing these moral sentiments to an origin in sympathy, which he takes to be an instinctive tendency to share the feelings of others. His disagreements with Hume are rather about the detailed way in which sympathy brings about these results. Whereas Hume stresses our sympathy with people in general, with society, and so bases our approval of the artificial virtues in particular on our knowledge of the utility of the system of conduct which they maintain, Smith stresses rather our sympathy with the person or persons principally involved. 'Whatever is the passion which arises from any object in the person principally concerned, an analogous emotion springs up, at the thought of his situation, in the breast of every attentive spectator.' But sympathy also operates in reverse; there is a corresponding tendency for the person principally involved to tone down his emotions to bring them into line with those of the spectators. These two operations of sympathy give rise to two kinds of virtue: 'the soft, the gentle, the amiable virtues' are based on the sympathy of spectators with those principally concerned; 'the great, the awful and respectable, the virtues of self-denial, of self-government ...' are based on the sympathy of the persons principally involved with the spectators. The various passions of human nature 'seem proper and are approved of, when the heart of every impartial spectator entirely sympathizes with them, when every indifferent by-stander entirely enters into, and goes along with them'. (Of course, 'indifferent' here does not mean that the bystander feels no concern, but only that he is not initially involved and

130

is therefore impartial as between those who are.) Smith explains that this is not just a matter of sharing the actual feelings of the persons involved. For example, if someone has been killed, he has no feelings for us to share; but we think of his having been deprived of life when he would have preferred to go on living, and so can feel resentment on his behalf (765–9).

Smith distinguishes the sense of 'the propriety of conduct' from that of its 'merit'. The sense of the propriety arises from a 'direct sympathy' with the affections and motives of the agent, that of the merit from an 'indirect sympathy' with the gratitude of the person acted upon, and the sense of demerit and impropriety are explained correspondingly (797–8). We apply these sentiments to our own conduct in the same way, examining it 'as we imagine any other fair and impartial spectator would examine it'. But, of course, we often fail to judge our own conduct impartially. In particular we tend to favour ourselves unfairly before we act; afterwards, when it is too late, we can more easily 'identify ourselves ... with the ideal man within the breast' and view both our situation and our conduct 'with the severe eyes of the most impartial spectator'. Smith bases on this fact an ingenious argument against the hypothesis that we have a *special* moral sense, an independent faculty of moral judgment. If we had this, since our own passions would be more immediately exposed to its view, 'it would judge with more accuracy concerning them, than concerning those of other men, of which it had only a more distant prospect.' But this does not happen. We are very prone to self-deceit; which 'is the source of half the disorders of human life. If we saw ourselves in the light in which others see us, or in which they would see us if they knew all, a reformation would generally be unavoidable. We could not otherwise endure the sight' (800, 812–16). The argument in this passage (perhaps the source of the phrase Burns made famous[1]), though ingenious, is not conclusive. Someone who believed in a special moral faculty could argue that its judgments may be clouded and distorted by self-interest even when its objects are in full view. On the other hand Smith can argue that it is both unnecessary and implausible to postulate a special moral sense, since the phenomena of moral judgment are better explained by the complex operations of sympathy. In particular he points out that there is no real resemblance between our feelings when we approve of a kindly sentiment and when we approve of a courageous one. There is not a single moral emotion which is aroused by each; rather in each case what is called approval is our entering, by sympathy, into the sentiment in question. Similarly,

131

Our horror for cruelty has no sort of resemblance to our contempt for mean-spiritedness. It is quite a different species of discord which we feel at the view of those two different vices, between our minds and those of the person whose sentiments and behaviour we consider. (840)

However, the crucial question is whether sympathy can explain our acceptance of general rules by which to judge conduct. Smith thinks that by learning of the sentiments of others which agree with our own about the actions of a third party, our own sentiments are reinforced and made more uniform, and so are more readily applied to our own conduct, overcoming our initial resistance to this. I think he is also suggesting that having found that the sentiments of others agree with our own about a third party, we get into the habit of agreeing with the sentiments of others, and so are more afraid of having them applied adversely to our own actions. But he insists that a body of similar approvals and disapprovals in similar particular cases precedes and gives rise to general rules; we do not first formulate the rules and then apply them to particular cases (816–17).

But I do not think that this is an adequate explanation. What Smith is doing is to elaborate and improve the psychological explanation of our moral thinking which Hume offers in the sections about the natural virtues. Even thus improved, however, it is not enough on its own. We can and must add to this explanation the advantage, to each of a number of self-interested and partly competitive persons, of there being rules which check conflict and encourage a certain amount of mutual aid, and the possibility of developing such rules as conventions by way of pressures that people can put on one another. Only when we add this sociological component do we have an explanation of the growth of moral attitudes which makes it unnecessary to postulate a special moral sense or faculty.

Whereas Adam Smith is, on the fundamental issues, an ally of Hume, Richard Price is an opponent. He sees very clearly the subjectivism of Hutcheson's account of moral sense:

it is evident, he considered it as the effect of a *positive constitution* of our minds, or as an *implanted* and *arbitrary* principle by which a *relish* is given us for certain moral objects and forms and aversion to others ... our ideas of morality, if this account is right, have the same origin with our ideas of the sensible qualities of bodies [that is, the secondary qualities], the harmony of sounds, or the beauties of

132

painting or sculpture; that is, the mere good pleasure of our Maker adapting the mind and its organs in a particular manner to certain objects. Virtue ... is an affair of taste. Moral right and wrong, signify nothing *in the objects themselves* to which they are applied, any more than agreeable and harsh; sweet and bitter; pleasant and painful; but only *certain effects in us*.

He explicitly makes this contrast between subjectivism and objectivism the central issue:

> The present inquiry therefore is; whether this be a true account of virtue or not; whether it *has* or *has not* a foundation in the *nature* of its object; whether *right* and *wrong* are real characters of *actions*, or only qualities of our *minds*; whether, in short, they denote what actions *are*, or only sensations derived from the particular frame and structure of our natures. (657)

It is true that these remarks fail to formulate the issue accurately, since only a crude or confused variant of sentimentalism would say simply that rightness and wrongness are qualities of our minds, and no variant of sentimentalism would deny that moral distinctions have *some* foundation in the natures of their objects, that the things we approve of are intrinsically different from those we condemn; for example, kind actions are different from cruel ones. Yet on a charitable reading Price can be taken to be indicating the crucial issue between sentimentalism as such and its rivals, whether there are or are not objectively prescriptive features with categorically imperative force.[2]

Price criticizes 'schemes which found morality on self-love, on positive laws and compacts, or the divine will'. These, he says, must either mean that moral terms are synonymous with words like 'advantageous', 'disadvantageous', 'willed', and 'forbidden', or else they deal not with the question 'what is the nature and true *account* of virtue but, what is the *subject-matter* of it'. Like G. E. Moore,[3] Price is rightly insisting that it is one question to ask what things are good and quite another to ask what goodness itself is − and similarly with any other moral features. It might be that producing happiness, for example, is right; but that is not to say that its rightness consists in its production of happiness, that to be right is simply to produce happiness, or that 'right' merely means 'producing happiness'. If this were so, then the statement that producing happiness is right would be a trifling tautology, which it plainly is not. Similarly, if obligation were simply *the necessity of doing a*

133

thing in order to be happy, the proposition that one is obliged to study one's own happiness would be trivial. Price thus repeatedly uses what has come to be known, in relation to Moore's work, as the open question argument; not that Price originated it: for example, Hutcheson uses it too (658, 718, 350–1).

Having thus isolated the characteristic moral predicates, Price asks what power within us perceives the distinction of right and wrong, and answers, 'the understanding', that is, the faculty that makes judgments and discerns truth. In saying this, he is opting firmly for the view that moral features are objective. To defend this claim, he argues that the understanding 'is a spring of new ideas' – new simple ideas – contrary to what Locke and his empiricist followers have believed. It is the understanding, not the senses, that compares the objects of the different senses with one another, that observes in them '*essence, number, identity, diversity*, etc.', and that decides that sounds and colours (as we perceive them) are not '*properties of external substances*' but '*modifications of our souls*'. Price also argues that our ideas of solidity, inertia, substance, duration, space, infinity, power, causation, and the distinction between necessity and possibility or contingency are all due to the understanding. His thought is that once we have recognized that the understanding, in these other cases, is an independent source of information about objective reality, we shall have little reason to deny that it is working similarly in giving us the basic ideas of moral value. And he thinks that if we did not recognize this, since the senses alone cannot give us these various ideas or knowledge of the associated truths, for example that every new event requires some cause, we should be plunged into an 'abyss of scepticism' (659–68).

Now it is obvious that these different notions which Price ascribes to the understanding are not all alike; we need a number of distinct accounts of how we develop them and of why we are justified, if we are, in employing them in our description of the external world. But whatever we say about this, there is still a profound disanalogy between all these features and the supposed moral qualities of right and wrong. This lies in the fact on which Hume's main argument in III i 1 is based, that these moral qualities are thought to supply immediate, unconditional, directives to action, which is not done by any of the metaphysical features in Price's list. Price, indeed, instructively mishandles this topic. Hutcheson had insisted that 'election' or 'approbation', our pro-attitude towards something, can be defined only trivially, by synonyms, and cannot be reduced to anything else (358).

134

Price turns this into the claim that our ideas of right and wrong are simple ideas. He thereby abandons Clarke's view that moral features can be arrived at by some kind of reasoning; instead they must, in at least some cases, somehow be immediately perceived. But *what* is it that is immediately perceived? If Price's objectivity thesis is correct, then these moral features must be something in the possible actions which, when perceived, carries Hutcheson's 'election' and 'approbation' with it. They can be, if not defined, at least described in terms of the introspectively recognizable acts or attitudes of choice and approval with which they are, in some mysterious way, necessarily connected. It is not really plausible to say even that election is unanalysable; but to transfer this claim to a supposed objective moral quality is to make its connection with choice and action utterly obscure (672).

Price makes three points in favour of his objectivity thesis. First, he says that Hutcheson's arguments against Clarke show only that moral features cannot be introduced by demonstration, but this leaves it open that they may be genuinely objective features, discerned by a faculty which discerns truth, not merely an 'implanted sense'; Hume's doctrine that ideas must be derived from impressions, and Locke's that they are all deducible from sensation and reflection, are unproved dogmas. Locke's attempt actually to derive the moral ideas plainly fails: it represents rectitude as conformity to rules or laws, which would make it absurd for us to ascribe rectitude, as we do, to rules and laws themselves, and to suppose God's will to be directed by it (674–5).

Secondly, he appeals to common sense and our knowledge of our own perceptions.

> It is scarcely conceivable that anyone can impartially attend to the nature of his own perceptions, and determine that, when he thinks gratitude or beneficence to be *right*, he perceives nothing *true* of them, and *understands* nothing, but only receives an impression from a sense.

Just as we know that equality is an objective feature that lines or figures may have, and that anyone who perceives the objects themselves (accurately enough) must perceive that they are equal, we have a like consciousness that we discern rightness in certain objects. We must admit that the actions of reasonable beings in promoting happiness are 'really right'. Correspondingly, certain things appear wrong; what reason have we for doubting that they really are wrong? (676–9)

However, Price realizes that this appeal is not conclusive:

It would, I doubt, be to little purpose to plead further here, the natural and universal apprehensions of mankind, that our ideas of right and wrong belong to the understanding, and denote real characters of actions; because it will be easy to reply, that they have a like opinion of the *sensible qualities* of bodies; and that nothing is more common than for men to mistake their own sensations for the properties of the objects producing them, or to apply to the object itself, what they find always accompanying it, when observed.

In other words, the apparent objectivity of moral features may be a systematic mistake, like the apparent objectivity of colours as we see them. So Price is well aware of what I called (in chapter V) the objectification theory as a variant of sentimentalism, and sees that it is a forceful counter to any appeal to common sense on behalf of moral objectivism. (This fact lends weight to my earlier suggestion that Hume at times adopted the objectification theory.) But Price thinks that he can reply to this argument. He claims that there is a sheer absurdity in the objectification of colours as we see them: 'A *coloured body*, if we speak accurately, is the same absurdity with a *square sound*. We need no experiments to prove that heat, cold, colours, tastes, etc. are not real qualities of bodies; because the ideas of matter and of the qualities, are incompatible.' By contrast, he thinks, there is no such incompatibility between *actions* and *right* (680–1).

However, the situation is the very reverse of what Price claims it to be. Perhaps he has an idea of matter such that the suggestion that it is coloured involves a contradiction; but that idea is itself the offspring of scientific theory. It did require experiments to establish the status of secondary qualities; there was no *a priori* incompatibility between what we initially knew about material objects and their having colours as we see colours. On the other hand it is very hard to see how a possible action could have such a property as the indefinable but action-guiding rightness or wrongness is supposed to be.

The alleged disanalogy between moral qualities and secondary qualities is Price's third point. If it fails, as I believe it does, he must fall back on a simple appeal to ordinary beliefs.

In short; it seems sufficient to overthrow any scheme, that such consequences, as the following, should rise from it: That no one being can judge one end to be better than another, or believe a real moral difference between actions; without giving his assent to an

136

impossibility; without mistaking the *affections of his own mind* for *truth*, and *sensation* for *knowledge*. (683)

On the contrary, this paradoxical implication of Hutcheson's sentimentalism, or Hume's, or Smith's is not enough to overthrow it. Price is right in his account of what moral judging *seems* to be, but this shows, not that sentimentalism is mistaken, but that the only defensible variant of sentimentalism is the objectification theory.

Although his main theme is the defence of objectivism, Price makes a curious concession to sentimentalism. Our intellectual faculties are, he says, in their infancy. Consequently 'in men it is necessary that the rational principle, or the *intellectual discernment* of *right* and *wrong*, should be aided by *instinctive determinations*.' Our maker has annexed sensations and instincts to our intellectual perceptions. So, misquoting Butler, Price says that 'in contemplating the actions of moral agents we have both a *perception of the understanding*, and a *feeling of the heart*', and that the latter depends partly on 'the positive constitution of our natures', but also, and principally, 'on the essential congruity or incongruity between moral ideas and our intellectual faculties'. But what this congruity or incongruity can be, or how feelings could result from it, is utterly obscure (688).

Price follows Butler in saying that beneficence is not the whole of virtue, and that such duties as gratitude, veracity, and justice (in the sense of honesty with regard to property) are independently obligatory (730). He argues explicitly against any purely utilitarian analysis or explanation of morality. The rewarding of virtue and the punishing of vice tend, he agrees, to prevent misery and to increase happiness, but 'that is not *all* that renders such a procedure right. ... Vice is of ESSENTIAL DEMERIT; and virtue is *in itself rewardable*' (697). God would want to make good men happier than bad men, quite apart from any further effects of such a distribution; his end is 'not simply happiness, but "happiness enjoyed with virtue" '. That is, Price ascribes to God, and to our ordinary moral consciousness, and adopts himself, a partly retributive theory of reward and punishment.[4] Similarly he argues that rights cannot be explained simply in terms of general utility:[5]

if publick good be the sole measure and foundation of *property* and of the *rights* of beings, it would be absurd to say *innocent* beings have a right to exemption from misery, or that they may not be made in any degree miserable, if but the smallest degree of *prepollent* good can arise from it.

F

Price is right in saying that our ordinary moral judgments are not *derived* from utilitarian considerations. Whether they could be *reconciled* with utilitarian principles and *justified* in terms of them, given the ordinary circumstances of human life, is more controversial.[6] He is right also about the content of our ordinary moral beliefs and concepts, particularly in claiming that to see some possible action as morally right, as realizing the relevant virtue or virtues, is to see this as *in itself* a reason for doing it, and correspondingly that wrongness would be *in itself* a reason for not doing something. But this still leaves room for a further explanation of why we have these concepts, and an account based on Hume's notion of the gradual development of conventions can explain even the non-utilitarian elements. Retributive principles result when instinctive tendencies of gratitude and resentment are developed into an interpersonal system of objectified moral characterizations. Rights result similarly when competing individual claims generate a convention not only of observing a compromise between those claims but of endorsing the adjusted claims from a general point of view, and ultimately of objectifying them. Price's explanation of justice, as contrasted with his correct report of the content of our beliefs, is comparatively shallow. 'An object, it is obvious, will acquire the relation to a person which has been mentioned, in consequence of first possession; in consequence of its being the fruit of his labour; by donation, succession, and in many other ways not necessary to be here enumerated' (742). The relation mentioned is simply one that implies that it is fit that the person should have the disposal of the object rather than other persons, and that it is wrong to deprive him of it. In other words, Price thinks that the conventional rules of property-holding and property-acquisition together are self-evidently valid. But Hume's detailed argument in III ii 3 shows that they are not. Again, Price assimilates promise-keeping to veracity, as Warnock has recently done.[7] In keeping a promise you make a statement true by making the fact agree with the statement, whereas in ordinary truth-telling you make the statement agree with the fact (739–40). But this account misses most of the point of promise-keeping and fails to explain the great importance commonly assigned to it – much greater than that commonly assigned to truth-telling. If fidelity to promises is taken as a species of veracity, it must at least be seen as involving certain further relations to human purposes which make this sort of veracity peculiarly pressing, which make it the object of unusually strong demands. But I do not see how this point can be worked out except by basing the obligation to keep a promise either on some utilitarian principle or on a convention of the sort that is indicated by Hume's theory of the artificial virtues. The weakness of Price's detailed explanation of the various virtues, such as honesty and fidelity, compared with the kind of explanation that can be developed if we follow Hume's notion of a convention and the indirect operation of initially conflicting purposes, must help to discredit the general intuitionist theory within whose framework they are stated, correct though this is as a *description* of our moral concepts.

On the other hand Price shows clearly how Wollaston's argument fails, anticipating the second of the two criticisms I used against it in chapter II: such expressions as 'treating things as they are', 'congruity and incongruity between actions and relations', and so on 'are of no use ... if considered as intended to *define* virtue, for they evidently *presuppose* it. Treating an object as being what *it is*, is treating it as *it is right such* an object should be treated' (726).

Thomas Reid's position is close to that of Price. Like him he abandons the attempt to introduce moral features by demonstration. Moral reasoning, like any other kind of reasoning, needs first principles, but he claims that these are self-evident; they are objective moral truths perceived by 'an original power of the mind' (879). We can see, in the advance from the views of Clarke and Wollaston, in response to the criticisms of Hutcheson and Hume, to the views of Price and Reid, the gradual realization of an important constraint on objectivism in morals: what is distinctively moral, in so far as it is prescriptive, cannot be introduced by any reasoning that works on purely non-prescriptive elements; if it is not supplied by something that falls under the heading of 'sentiment', there must somewhere be a direct intellectual apprehension of some distinctively moral truths. In this sense any coherent objectivism about the prescriptive aspect of morality must be intuitionist. But of course this does not entail that all moral thinking is just a matter of having isolated intuitions. It is only some first principles or data that the objectivist must claim to be intuitively known, and these might be either general principles or judgments of any degree of specificity or a mixture of the two; reasoning of various sorts, deductive or inductive or hypothesis-confirming, could proceed from these. But some directly known prescriptive principles are required, and this is a fundamental and inescapable problem for moral objectivism.

Again like Price, Reid says that duty, for example, is indefinable, except trivially by synonymous terms. But he carefully specifies its category and its location: duty or moral obligation is a relation between an agent and an action; this must be a voluntary action of the agent himself, who must have the means of knowing his obligation, and the moral description of any action depends upon 'the opinion of the agent in doing it' (869, 873–5).

But Reid also makes a counter-attack on Hume, arguing that it is only by misusing the word 'reason' that he has been able to claim that reason is inert. What we ordinarily mean by 'reason' includes the pursuit of ends which can be conceived only by beings endowed with reason, and of which, without reason, we could not even form a conception, namely *our good on the whole* and *our duty*. The very notion of what is good or bad for us on the whole, he argues, involves our taking an extended view of our lives, past, present, and future, reflecting on the consequences of past actions and the likely consequences of future ones. So this conception is 'the offspring of reason', and if it gives rise to any principle of action in man, that 'may very properly be called a rational principle of action'; and regard to duty is another rational principle of action (860–8).

However, this argument is of no value as a reply to Hume. We can agree that the words 'reason', 'reasonable', 'rational' and so on are commonly used to distinguish prudent from impulsive or shortsighted actions, and hence also to identify or characterize the prudential motive, concern for one's good on the whole. We can also concede that this motive presupposes the use of what even Hume would call 'reason'. But all this leaves Hume's real point untouched. Admittedly one could not have the prudential purpose without the 'reason' (in Hume's sense). But the crucial claim would be the converse of this, that one could not have the 'reason' without the prudential purpose, that the comparing of experiences, collecting of information, estimating of consequences, and perceiving of connections between different phases of my life, which together make up the reasoning that underlies the conception of my good on the whole, can in itself direct me to pursue that good or to take it as an end. There are, indeed, two thoughts which may appear to support this claim. One is that a person would be unlikely to engage in this congeries of reasoning processes if he did not also have the prudential motive: all this reflecting and comparing naturally goes along with concern for one's good on the whole, and would lack point if one had no such concern. Also, motivation enters into the various items which are compared or weighed against one another, so that it is not surprising that such a rational process should issue in a further (though new and distinct) motivation. But this second thought is just a tempting confusion. The conclusion Reid wants, that my good on the whole is a rational end, includes a direction to give equal weight to present and future desires, or to nearer or remoter satisfactions, and there is nothing in the present and expected future motives themselves that will yield, through rational comparison and calculation, any such direction. It is true (and this is the first of our thoughts again) that one is unlikely to compare nearer and remoter satisfactions fairly and clearsightedly unless one is at the same time giving them equal motivational weight; but we can and must distinguish this fact sharply from the quite unwarranted suggestion that such a comparison, in so far as it yields knowledge or truth, rationally requires this equal motivational weight and makes my good on the whole a rational end. 'Reason' in Hume's sense and the prudential motive are indeed causally intertwined in a manner which makes natural the common use of the word 'reason' which Reid stresses; it is for most purposes convenient to have a word that signifies this causal complex of intellectual and motivational elements. But the intellectual and the motivational aspects can be distinguished, and it is simply a confusion to suppose that the intellectual aspect rationally requires the motivational, though it is true that the motivational aspect necessarily presupposes the intellectual.

Analogous criticisms apply to any corresponding attempt to show that regard for one's duty is a rational principle of action in the sense Reid requires. Reid does not in fact base the conception of duty on a reflective comparison of the interests of all human beings or all rational agents, as the conception of one's good on the whole is based on a reflective comparison of all the interests (including future interests) of this human being. But even if he had done so, we could only have concluded that our having this conception, and *a fortiori* our having a regard for our duty so conceived, requires reasoning, not that reasoning in any sense in which it establishes truths requires that we should have this regard for duty.

Reid does, indeed, make one good point against Hume in this area: 'there may be conviction without passion; and the conviction of what we ought to do, in order to some end which we have judged fit to be pursued, is what I call a *rational motive*' (887). That is, the mere *firm belief* that something is fit to be pursued, and that such fitness is an objective requirement to act, can be a motive to action without any accompanying passion or desire, as we noted in chapter IV. Hume's psychological thesis is overstated if he claims that motivation always involves a desire as well as belief. The belief in objective moral requirements, made explicit by such writers as Clarke and Price and Reid, but implicit in much ordinary moral thinking, can in this curious way act as a motive on its own, even if, as Hume would argue, that belief is false. But though Reid may *call* this a rational motive, what would be needed to make it rational in any important sense is that the belief in question should be true.

On this central issue Reid can do little more than Price. He argues that sensation or feeling is often 'inseparably conjoined' with judgment or belief. 'When we perceive an external object by our senses, we have a sensation conjoined with a firm belief of the existence and sensible qualities of the external object' (914–15). Here the belief is a consequence of the sensation, but Reid has elsewhere defended commonsense realism about the external world, and therefore holds that such beliefs are justified. But in other cases where belief and feeling are combined, notably the moral ones, the feeling is a consequence of the judgment, the judgment being partly about the non-moral facts, but partly a moral judgment as well. For example, I feel love or esteem for a man who seems to be exerting himself in a good cause; but the feeling changes if I am persuaded that he was bribed, or 'acted from some mercenary or bad motive' (917). But again Reid's appeal is simply to our introspective view of what we are doing when we judge morally.

> When I exercise my moral faculty about my own actions or those of other men, I am conscious that I judge as well as feel. I accuse and excuse, I acquit and condemn, I assent and dissent, I believe and disbelieve and doubt. These are acts of judgement, and not feelings. Every determination of the understanding, with regard to what is true or false, is judgement. That I ought not to steal, or to kill, or to bear false witness, are propositions, of the truth of which I am as well convinced as of any proposition in Euclid. I am conscious that I judge them to be true propositions; and my consciousness makes all other arguments unnecessary, with regard to the operations of my own mind. That other men judge, as well as feel, in such cases, I am convinced, because they understand me when I express my moral judgement, and express theirs by the same terms and phrases. (918)

In other words, my own moral determinations seem to me to be judgments, and what seems to me to be a judgment of my own must be so; and the interpersonal use of language is as good a warrant here for assuming that there is genuine communication with sameness of meaning between speakers as it is in any other field.

142

In this Reid is surely right, and this is enough decisively to rule out non-cognitivist (emotivist or prescriptivist) views if they are offered as a conceptual analysis of moral thinking or as accounts of the standard meaning of moral statements. Equally, Reid's argument rules out all the dispositional descriptivist variants of sentimentalism, for although they take moral determinations to be genuine judgments, they reduce them to judgments about how this or that observer would react to the actions in question, while introspection of the sort to which Reid is appealing shows clearly that this is not what we ordinarily take our own moral determinations to be about, and his point about linguistic communication extends this to the judgments of others. But Reid's argument does not show that the judgments we make are objective in the sense that the distinctively moral properties they ascribe to actions are ever really found in them: it is powerless against the objectification variant of sentimentalism.

Reid sums up his argument thus:

> This doctrine, therefore, that moral approbation is merely a feeling without judgement, necessarily carries along with it this consequence, that a form of speech, upon one of the most common topics of discourse, which either has no meaning, or a meaning irreconcilable to all rules of grammar or rhetoric, is found to be common and familiar in all languages and in all ages of the world, while every man knows how to express the meaning, if it have any, in plain and proper language. Such a consequence I think sufficient to sink any philosophical opinion on which it hangs. (924)

He also makes another 'ordinary language' point against Hume. The word 'sentiment' is commonly used to refer to items that conjoin feeling and judgment in the way that Reid rightly sees to be characteristic of a great deal of our thinking. But Hume uses it to mean feeling alone. Thus readers who agree that morality is – as indeed it is – a matter of sentiments in the ordinary sense may be tricked into accepting his conclusion that it is a matter of feeling alone (927). However, Hume, especially in the *Enquiry*, makes it clear that he does not think that morality is a matter of feeling *alone*. Various operations which he would put under the heading of 'reason' come in, but play a subordinate role. In any case, his view that what he calls 'the final sentence' depends essentially upon feeling is supported by arguments, not by a mere verbal trick or ambiguity.

Reid can and does show that all the terms commonly used in morals 'necessarily imply judgement in their meaning', and he effectively satirizes a simple version of sentimentalism:[8]

> Let us apply this reasoning to the office of a judge. In a case that comes before him, he must be made acquainted with all the objects, and all their relations. After this, his understanding has no farther room to operate. Nothing remains, on his part, but to feel the right or the wrong; and mankind have, very absurdly, called him a *judge*; he ought to be called a *feeler*. (928, 936)

Such arguments do indeed prove that moral approbation is not *just* feeling without judgment. But there is a variant of sentimentalism which they cannot sink. Our ordinary moral judgments are indeed judgments, grammatically and conceptually. In part they ascribe to actions and characters both qualities and relations which they may indeed have, the 'natural' features on which the moral descriptions supervene. But they go beyond such natural descriptions to claim that, as a matter of objective truth, certain things must or must not be done, that there are objective requirements for or against possible actions, and hence also for or against the dispositions that would give rise to and be seen to be realized in such actions. Here what are ascribed are illusory features, and the illusion is generated in a complicated way by the interplay of our sentiments in social situations in which the illusion, once established and regularly employed in interpersonal communication and shared opinions, can play an important and perhaps a useful part.

I conclude, therefore, that though Price and Reid are very able and clear-headed critics and persuasive debaters, they can make little headway against Hume's important doctrines. They rather confirm those doctrines by the ineffectiveness of their criticisms. Hume's most striking moral theses are opposed and severely tested by some of his successors, but they can be interpreted in such a way that they are able to survive these tests.

IX

CONCLUSIONS

Four main points emerge from our survey of the long debate from
Hobbes to Reid, and are fairly firmly established by it. First, that the only
coherent objectivism in ethics would be some form of intuitionism, such
as Price and Reid fall back on, abandoning the more extravagant claims
of Clarke and Wollaston. Secondly, that the only plausible variant of
sentimentalism is the objectification theory. Thirdly, that this variant
needs to be expanded, somewhat as Hume expands it, into a sociological
theory of artificial virtues based on conventions, which can be seen as
arising out of the game theory problems, particularly of the partial
conflict sort, to which Hobbes drew attention; but this approach needs
to be applied also to some features of what Hume classes as natural
virtues. Fourthly, that when sentimentalism is thus interpreted and
developed, it can explain the paradoxes which it admittedly involves,
and gives a better explanation of moral thinking as a whole than even a
coherent, intuitionist, objectivism.

However, each of the four needs to be made more precise, and I want
also to say something about three further questions. To what extent is
our conclusion a vindication of those views of Hobbes which started this
debate? In what sense, if any, is Hume's theory a utilitarian one? And,
finally, have I been right in the previous chapters to follow Hume in
regarding morality itself as useful or beneficial, as fulfilling a social
function, or should it be seen rather as doing more harm than good?

There are two sides of the intuitionism which is the only coherent
objectivist moral theory. The first is the thesis that there are some basic
moral principles, not themselves establishable by reasoning or derivable
by reasoning from any collection of non-moral truths, unless the

reasoning relies either on special derivation rules which are tantamount to additional, specifically moral, premisses or (like Searle's derivation of *ought* from *is*) on clusters of linguistic rules which, as clusters, implicitly incorporate categorical imperatives. But what, in the supposedly objective moral truths, is thus not constructable and not derivable from ordinary or 'natural' components is just the categorically imperative element. The coherent intuitionist thesis is just that there must occur somewhere in sound moral thinking an injection of something categorically imperative. The second aspect of intuitionism is the ascription of the knowledge that this categorically imperative element is objectively valid to a 'special cognitive faculty'. But this needs to be interpreted with some care. Within some action, for example, which (on the present hypothesis) is correctly morally characterized as, say, wrong, it must be possible in principle to distinguish the directive element, the fact that this action is not to be done, from all the other, 'natural' features, especially from what it is about it that makes it wrong. But it may be denied that we can draw this distinction. It may be argued that we often do not possess concepts through which we can recognize and describe these relevant natural features in isolation from their wrongness. It is already in contexts of evaluation and commendation and condemnation that we learn to pick out and recognize thoughtfulness or cowardice or meanness: we do not first learn to classify actions or dispositions under purely 'descriptive' headings by reference to their purely 'natural' features, and then add a further, separate, evaluation, this being, on the present hypothesis, the work of a special faculty. But whether this is so or not does not matter. Even if in practice we always learn to recognize the aspect of moral value and the natural features connected with it together, there must be such features and they must be distinguishable in principle. Surely we can imagine a sufficiently acute but value-blind Martian anthropologist finding out just what it is that we classify as thoughtfulness or cowardice or meanness. Of course these natural features will include the mental states of the people involved in the actions, and some of these may be beliefs about objective moral requirements. These beliefs may, on the present hypothesis, be true; but our Martian will not himself see them as true or endorse their objects as requirements, though if he is fully to understand our classification of actions, to grasp the *natural* features that make them count as right or wrong in various ways, he must understand the content of those beliefs. Though they may include such complexities, these natural features must, then, be distinguishable in principle.

Further, on the present hypothesis, the rightness or wrongness must supervene in a regular, universal, way upon the relevant natural features: it could not be that of two actions whose natural features were exactly alike one was morally permissible and the other morally wrong. Now the 'special faculty' is needed to detect this necessary supervenience of, say, an action's wrongness, the fact that it is not to be done, upon the complete set of its natural features. But if we, unlike the value-blind Martian, never get a conceptual grip on the relevant members of this set of natural features in isolation from the wrongness, we shall never be in the position of explicitly detecting the supervenience as such. We may have acquired the complex moral concept as a whole, getting the wrong-making features into focus only in conjunction with the wrongness; and once we have this concept no special faculty will be needed to enable us to apply it; ordinary methods of observation (including psychological insight) will suffice. In fact what will be going on is that our ordinary perceptual capacities will be responding to the relevant natural features, but since these are, as we might say, *index-linked*, conceptualized only along with a certain direction, with their categorically imperative wrongness, we shall have the impression that we discover the whole moral quality of the action in one go, by ordinary methods of observation. Nevertheless, on the objectivist hypothesis which we are now clarifying there is knowledge of a synthetic necessary truth of supervenience built into our possession of the complex moral concept, and *that* knowledge has not been given by ordinary observation. This is what must be ascribed to the 'special faculty of moral intuition' if it is claimed to be *knowledge*, even though to speak in this way is to interpret what is going on rather than simply to describe moral experience as we ordinarily have it.[1] And even here there is no need to think of this 'special faculty' as a separate organ of the mind. As Price says, all that is needed is that the understanding, the aspect of our minds which can discover objective truths, *has the ability* to discover, among others, this particular sort of necessary truth of supervenience.

Turning now from this objectivist hypothesis to its sentimentalist rival, we can see that the suggested 'objectification' applies particularly to that same element of (now merely apparent) categorical imperativeness which was isolated above as the object of a supposed special cognitive faculty. The natural features we distinguished from this are uncontroversially objective already. But we must guard against too simple an interpretation of the 'objectification'. What is objectified is not just a feeling that happens to be there. The objectifying must be understood in conjunction with the process by which the artificial virtues are developed – and, in our correction of Hume's account, all the virtues are at least partly artificial.

This process has to explain, for each virtue, both a practice and an approval tendency, a disposition to act in certain ways and positively to refrain from acting in others, and a tendency to approve of the former ways of acting and to disapprove of the latter. The practice and the approval tendency encourage and help one another, but we also need to account for the two together. In principle at least five sorts of explanation might be offered. One is that these are the result of a process of biological evolution, natural selection having favoured certain inheritable tendencies which helped the individuals who had them to survive and reproduce. A second substitutes cultural for biological evolution: culture traits or 'memes'[2] can similarly reproduce themselves and may be selected for survival, and this process can operate within a shorter time-span than is usually needed for significant changes through biological evolution. A third explanation is that the practice, at least, is deliberately adopted by those who participate in it through intelligent calculation with a view to their individual well-being. In adopting the practice, they would also automatically recommend it to themselves and to one another; but the sentiment of approval, in so far as it goes beyond such calculated recommendation, would have to be explained in some other way. It might, perhaps, be explained, as Hume suggests, as resulting from instinctive sympathy and benevolence, while these in turn might be explained by our first or second account, as being due to biological or cultural evolution. A fourth explanation is that the practice is deliberately adopted with a view to the general happiness, the interest of society, but then the concern for this general interest would need to be explained in turn by benevolence and sympathy, and these by one or other sort of evolution. A fifth explanation is that a generally beneficial practice is developed by what, following Hume, we have called a convention, and is constantly recreated and maintained by reciprocal pressures between selfish (or only self-referentially altruistic) individuals. The recommending of the practice would again follow automatically, but the sentiment of approval would require, as before, some further explanation.

Of these five possible explanations, the first is being rejected by Hume when he speaks of artificial virtues. It may hold for some basic emotional and behavioural tendencies, pre-moral rather than moral, such as family affection, resentment of injuries, grudge-bearing, gratitude for benefits, love of human companionship, and perhaps (as Hume held) an inclination towards sympathy with any creatures seen as resembling oneself, producing some general benevolence, though variable in degree. But it will not account for honesty, fidelity to promises, political allegiance, or the virtues of veracity, beneficence, or even non-maleficence as applicable to all the other persons. These are not biologically determined in any direct way. The third explanation, in terms of calculated self-interest, though often mentioned explicitly by Hume (as also by Hobbes) can surely play only a minor and subordinate part. The fourth, in terms of calculated pursuit of the general interest, the well-being of society, can also have played only a small part: as Hume so effectively argued, if general benevolence had been strong enough to produce the artificial virtues in this direct way, it would have been so strong as to make them unnecessary. On the whole, then, we are left with the second explanation and the fifth, that is, with cultural evolution and conventions based on indirect self-love. Cultural evolution is not so easy an explanation as it might appear: there is no automatic connection between the fact that a practice is beneficial to a society in which it flourishes and any selective encouragement of that practice.[3] Still, it is true that beneficial memes can be selected in special circumstances, though an adequate explanation along these lines would require an account of some mechanism by which such selection takes place. The fifth explanation therefore gains in importance from the difficulties which, in varying degrees, affect all its rivals. Recognizably moral practices should be seen as being continually recreated and maintained by reciprocal pressures. And whereas Hume gave a different explanation (based on sympathy and concern for the well-being of society) for the associated approval tendencies, I see no reason why we cannot understand these moral sentiments also as being maintained by reciprocal pressures, though perhaps also reinforced in a number of ways. Mainly through processes of this fifth sort, therefore, but with some help from processes of the other four sorts, there has grown up and there is maintained an interpersonal system of practices that reflect established dispositions and of evaluations that combine the conceptual specification of various sorts of behaviour (and the associated dispositions) with sentiments favouring or opposing them. By 'objectification' we must therefore mean the taking of the *whole* of such evaluation, including the pressures for or against something which in fact stem from the sentiments involved, to be objectively valid or authoritative, where in fact all that is objective is the sets of index-linked features selected and focused upon in that system of evaluation. This account of a system of evaluation incorporates (and so neutralizes) the sound point made by Reid's satirical description of the Humean judge as a *feeler*. We do not normally reach a stage where all the natural features of the action and its circumstances are before us, and we then add a sentiment by a further step. Rather we work throughout with the concepts of an evaluative system in which the natural features are already index-linked. Nevertheless, in employing such a system and regarding it as authoritative for conduct we have implicitly engaged in a process of objectification: forces which in fact arise from the sentiments of the various people involved are taken to operate independently of any such sentiments.

Once we have thus clarified the rival intuitionist and sentimentalist hypotheses, it should be clear in what way the sentimentalist view offers the better overall explanation of the phenomenon of morality. The rival hypothesis is still saddled with the ontological extravagance and the epistemological implausibility of categorical imperatives supervenient upon the natural features and intellectually recognizable as thus supervenient. On the other hand the main initial difficulty for the sentimentalist view, its apparent conflict with the claim to objectivity which is implicit in ordinary moral concepts and in the grammar and natural logic of moral language, has been removed by the theory of objectification, while this in turn, as well as much of the detailed content of morality, is plausibly explained by an account, developed out of Hume's, of the artificial virtues, including some aspects of those which he classed as natural.

To what extent is this conclusion a vindication of Hobbes? His doctrine that men are completely selfish has been effectively criticized by many of his successors, and must be drastically modified. Nor have we found a need for an absolute political sovereign. Again, while Hobbes sees moral practices as being deliberately adopted through intelligent calculation as a means to individual well-being, this seems not to be their main explanation. These are radical corrections; yet after they have been made the main outlines of his theory still stand. He was right in denying objective moral qualities and relations. He was right in seeing morality as a solution to a social problem of partial conflict which is not solved, but rather made more acute, by human instincts and the ordinary human situation. He was largely right in his view of the form of the problem, and partly right in his identification of the elements to be used in a solution. But his notion of sovereignty exaggerates the part that has to be played by government, and his notion of covenants overstresses explicit agreement whereas more weight should be placed on the notion of convention that we have extracted from Hume's discussion and the mechanism of reciprocal sanctions. Though self-love (along with self-referential altruism) must still do most of the work, the socially beneficial moral structures are produced mainly by its *indirect* operation. In short, Hobbes's account is correct in outline, though wrong in some important details.

It will be obvious that my interpretation of Hume has brought him close to Hobbes. But there is plenty of backing for this interpretation in the text of the *Treatise*. I have merely made central the thesis which Hume states explicitly in III ii 6 that ' 'tis self-love which is their real origin' – that is, the real origin of the 'laws of justice' and presumably of the artificial virtues in general. 'This system', he adds, '... comprehending the interest of each individual, is of course advantageous to the public; tho' it be not intended for that purpose by the inventors'. Again 'There is no passion, therefore, capable of controlling the interested affection, but the very affection itself, by an alteration of its direction' (II ii 2); and there are many similar remarks.

On the other hand, it is clear that Hume also has affinities with Hutcheson, and in many places stresses the reality and the importance of benevolence. But while we can thus see him as holding views intermediate between those of Hobbes and of Hutcheson, it seems clear to me that in Book III of the *Treatise* as a whole he is closer to Hobbes than to Hutcheson. However, my judgment about this may be biased by my belief that the truth also about the origin of the artificial virtues, and the forces that sustain them, lies closer to Hobbes's views than to Hutcheson's, and that the same applies to some extent even to the natural virtues.

This leads on to the question whether or to what extent we can count Hume as a utilitarian. In the *Treatise*, at least, he is considerably less of a utilitarian than Hutcheson. Admittedly he holds that the virtues, natural and artificial alike, tend to promote utility or the public interest or the advantage of society – phrases which he uses repeatedly – though with the artificial ones it is only the 'whole system' that has this effect, not each virtuous act on its own. Admittedly he holds also that this is why these practices and dispositions are approved, why they count as virtues. But contribution to the general happiness is not the only feature that makes something a virtue: any 'quality of mind ... which is naturally fitted to be useful to others, or to the person himself, or which is agreeable to others, or to the person himself' will (through the operation of sympathy) give the right sort of pleasure, and so will count as a virtue (III iii 1). Since Hume is not concerned to put forward a normative thesis at all, he is, *a fortiori*, not saying that one ought to do whatever would maximize utility, or even that one ought to act in accordance with those rules, or to encourage and cultivate and display those dispositions, which are such as to maximize utility. The maximizing of utility, in fact, plays no part in his theory, even in his explanations of the practices we have or of our approval of them. Rather he is content to say that some practice (etc.) is in the public interest in contrast with some radically different alternative – for example, that it is better to have some government rather than none, or some stable property rules rather than none at all. The notions of a calculus of utility and of aiming at the greatest happiness of the greatest number, which are clearly foreshadowed by Hutcheson, are not taken up and developed by Hume. Hume repeatedly deprecates any enquiry about what would be the best way of distributing property or the best form of government or the best choice of rulers; though it is true that his argument in each case is that the public interest would actually be harmed by attempts to promote it in such detailed ways, because of the disputes and conflicts and insecurity that would result. Hume is sometimes reluctant to invoke utility even where he could do so with considerable plausibility: 'Thus ... there are, no doubt, motives of public interest for most of the rules which determine property; but I still suspect, that these rules are principally fix'd by the imagination, or the more frivolous properties of our thought and conception' (III ii 3, note).

Hume's view also contrasts with a utilitarian approach in that he insists in III ii 1, and still more strongly in III iii 1, that motives, and character as a durable system of motives, are the primary subjects of moral judgments, and not actions. Whereas the utilitarian typically sees the rightness of actions – their bearing on the general happiness – as the most important thing, and motives and character as mattering only as sources of right actions, Hume holds that actions are considered merely as signs of motives: 'Actions are, indeed, better indications of a character than words, or even wishes and sentiments; but 'tis only so far as they are such indications, that they are attended with love or hatred, praise or blame.'

It is, therefore, somewhat surprising that Bentham writes as follows, referring explicitly to the third Book of the *Treatise*:

That the foundations of all *virtue* are laid in *utility*, is there demon-

strated, after a few exceptions made, with the strongest force of
evidence: but I see not, any more than Helvetius saw, what need
there was for the exceptions. For my part, I well remember, no sooner
had I read that part of the work which touches on this subject than
I felt as if scales had fallen from my eyes. I then, for the first time,
learnt to call the cause of the people the cause of Virtue. (Note to
chapter I, §36 of *A Fragment on Government*)

In the *Enquiry*, on the other hand, there is much more emphasis on
utility. The proposition which Hume examines and defends there (in
section III, part i) is 'That public utility is the *sole* origin of justice'.
Referring to such conceivable changes in the conditions of human life as
extreme abundance, extreme necessity, perfect humanity, and perfect
malice, he says 'By rendering justice totally *useless*, you thereby totally
destroy its essence, and suspend its obligation upon mankind.' Similarly
(in section IV) 'the sole foundation of the duty of allegiance is the
advantage, which it procures to society, by preserving peace and order
among mankind', and the same holds for chastity and various other
matters: 'Common interest and utility beget infallibly a standard of right
and wrong among the parties concerned.' Even for benevolence 'a *part*,
at least, of its merit arises from its tendency to promote the interests of
our species, and bestow happiness on human society' (section II, part ii).
The origin of moral language is that we 'invent a peculiar set of terms, in
order to express those universal sentiments of censure or approbation,
which arise from humanity, or from views of general usefulness and its
contrary' (section IX, part i). Even here, however, Hume does not say
that what we approve from a general point of view must even coincide
with what would maximize the general happiness (nor, I think, would
he be right to say this), let alone that everything of which we approve is
approved wholly on the ground of its apparent general utility.[4]

Though Hume, in the *Enquiry*, still treats justice, allegiance, chastity,
and so on separately from benevolence, he no longer speaks of them as
artificial virtues, and he replaces the Hobbesian account of their
generation by the indirect working of self-love with the simpler and
looser thesis that they develop because they are useful to society. But this
is a much weaker explanation: we may well ask exactly *how* common
interest and utility beget infallibly a standard of right and wrong; the
account in the *Treatise* suggests an answer, but that in the *Enquiry* does
not.

In neither work does Hume have any explicit theory of how to measure utility, how to weigh advantages to some persons against disadvantages to others. Rather he tends to represent whatever he thinks to be in the public interest as being also in the long-term interest of each person on his own. But this is clearly not the case, at least if we take into account a more finely graded range of alternatives than those he usually considers. Though it may be in almost everyone's interest to have some property rules rather than none, different sets of property rules would be differentially advantageous to various groups of people. This is one of a number of considerations which cast some doubt on Hume's usual optimistic assumption that morality itself is, from everyone's point of view, a good thing.

We can take up this question, whether morality does more harm than good, with the help of a distinction drawn in section 2 of chapter VI. With regard both to agreement-keeping and to respect for property — and, no doubt, with regard to other topics as well — we can distinguish a basic practice established by convention and reciprocal sanctioning from the full system in which this basic practice is reinforced by moral feelings, or even partly replaced by what appear to be moral perceptions, by agents employing morally-loaded concepts of property, rights, and obligations, and responding to what seem to them to be immediate requirements of the situations in which they are. As I have said, these moral elements help to make adherence to the basic practice more thoroughly in the interest of almost all those involved, both by their direct operation and by making it easier to support the practice with legal sanctions as well, while at the same time, by supplying other motives, it makes the appeal to self-interest less vital. Still, a case can be made out for the view that though what I am calling the basic practice is beneficial, it would be better without the moral overlay. Where there are conflicts of interest — and partial conflicts occur all the time — it will be easier to reach a reasonable compromise between the competing parties if everyone sees the issue as just that, a partial conflict of interests, without the embroidery of rights and moral justification. Bentham, indeed, made a similar point in favour of the principle of utility as against all the principles adverse to it,[5] but it can be applied against the moralizing of issues in any style at all. Besides, the adding of moral overtones to practice will in general have a conservative tendency: it will tend to stabilize whatever differential advantages the various parties initially have. The particular rules that are adopted with regard to the acquisition and stability and transfer of possessions are likely to reflect neither utility (in the sense of the promotion of the general happiness) nor 'imagination' and the 'frivolous properties of our thought', but rather 'the advantage of the stronger'[6] – that is, the advantage of whatever groups have most power when the rules are being established – and that advantage is increased if the rules thus made are sanctified by the addition to them of moral concepts and feelings. Again, an agreement will be made only if it is at least to the apparent advantage of both parties, in relation to a baseline determined by their initial positions; but it will be more to the advantage of whichever party starts in the stronger bargaining position – Hobbes's covenant of permanent submission to a conqueror is only an extreme case of this principle. A strong moral requirement of fidelity to promises will tend to perpetuate advantages arising from such initial differences in strength, in contrast with a weaker or more flexible principle, such as is familiar in international contexts, that allows renegotiation of agreements when conditions change. Though government is better for most people than anarchy, governments are always liable to get out of hand, to exceed their useful functions and either become corrupt and tyrannical or engage in ruinous international adventures. Do not the moral overtones of the duty of allegiance, with the associated concepts of loyalty, patriotism, and the like and the automatic condemnation which they carry of rebels and traitors, facilitate the misuse of power, whereas a more cynical or pragmatic view of the authority of governments would help to keep their ambitions in check? Without morality there might, indeed, be more small-scale fighting; but war as we know it, organized on a national or on an international scale, would be impossible. Indeed, Hume himself warned against the moralizing of allegiance which kept the Jacobites loyal to a 'rightful king', and those whom he classed as 'seditious bigots' were undoubtedly inspired by their own strong moral beliefs.

In short, even if morality fulfils a social function, it also has side-effects some of which benefit some people at the expense of others, while others do more harm than good to almost everyone. But could we do without it? What would work, in its place? The obvious answer is, what I have called the basic practices without their moral overlay, supplemented by the social psychologist's techniques of conflict resolution.[7]

But there is a case for the other side. It is easiest to understand the techniques of conflict resolution working within an agreed framework of *prima facie* – not absolute – rights possessed by all the parties to an issue. To the argument that strong principles of fidelity to promises perpetuate initial advantages we can reply that what they do is to postpone the use of those advantages; without them anyone who has an initial advantage will be tempted to make the most of it at once, in ways that may be greatly to the detriment of his opponent. And moral considerations can be and often are invoked against privilege, against the strong, and against the misuse of power.

A thorough discussion of this question would be beyond the scope of this book. But it had to be raised, so that our account, largely following Hume's, of the social function of morality should not leave a misleadingly optimistic impression. In conclusion, I suggest that morality is less likely to have these regrettable side-effects if it is *understood*. What, as Hume saw, holds for the duty of allegiance holds also for morality as a whole. We are more likely to get its benefits without its disadvantages if we see through its claim to absolute or objective authority. Fundamentally, the human situation is one of partial conflict, which both calls for and admits of resolution, and morality is one device among others which can help to resolve or mitigate such conflicts.

NOTES

I INTRODUCTION: OUTLINE OF HUME'S THEORY

1 Books I and II of *A Treatise of Human Nature* were published in 1739, when Hume was twenty-seven, and Book III in 1740. His *Enquiry concerning the Principles of Morals*, a re-writing of Book III of the *Treatise*, appeared in 1751. Hume thought that the failure of the *Treatise* to attract much attention was due to its defects of style, and the *Enquiry* is certainly a much more polished work. But in improving the presentation of his moral theory Hume smoothed off too many corners, and softened or suppressed some of his most significant arguments. See chapter IX, pp. 151–3.

2 Cf. J. A. Passmore, *Hume's Intentions* (Cambridge, 1952), p. 43. For a full discussion of the relation between Hume's work and Newton's, see J. Noxon, *Hume's Philosophical Development* (Oxford, 1973).

II SOME PREDECESSORS: HOBBES, SHAFTESBURY, CLARKE, WOLLASTON, MANDEVILLE, HUTCHESON, BUTLER

1 This description of the debate is borrowed from the cover of *British Moralists 1650–1800*, edited by D. D. Raphael (Oxford, 1969).

2 References in this style, with numbers alone in parentheses, are to the marginally numbered sections in *British Moralists 1650–1800*.

3 See also T. Hobbes, *Leviathan*, chapter 15, paragraphs 5 to 9, chapter 21, paragraphs 8 and 9, chapter 26, especially paragraphs 10 and 40, chapter 27, and especially chapter 29.

4 The interpretation of Hobbes's moral position is the subject of controversy. For several contrasting views, see *Hobbes Studies*, edited by Keith C. Brown (Blackwell, Oxford, 1965). I am following the traditional or orthodox interpretation.

5 Cf. R. Dawkins, *The Selfish Gene* (Oxford, 1976).

6 Berkeley was very critical of Shaftesbury on the ground that his system is

157

implicitly atheistic, that it introduces 'taste instead of duty', and includes no motion of law, divine judgment, or a future state. 'So long as we admit no principle of good actions but natural affection, no reward but natural consequences; so long as we apprehend no judgment, harbour no fears, and cherish no hopes of a future state, but laugh at all these things, with the author of the *Characteristics*, and those whom he esteems the liberal and polished part of mankind, how can we be said to be religious in any sense?' See G. Berkeley, *The Theory of Vision Vindicated and Explained*.

7 Cf. my *Truth, Probability, and Paradox* (Oxford, 1973), chapter 2.
8 J. L. Austin, *How to do things with Words* (Oxford, 1962), Lecture I.
9 References in this style, with 'BM' followed by page numbers in parentheses, are to *British Moralists*, edited by L. A. Selby-Bigge (Oxford, 1897).
10 I. Kant, *Groundwork of the Metaphysic of Morals*, chapter 1.

III   HUME'S PSYCHOLOGY OF ACTION   (*TREATISE* II iii 3)

1 J. Harrison, *Hume's Moral Epistemology* (Oxford, 1976), p. 5.

IV   MORALITY NOT BASED ON REASON   (*TREATISE* III i 1)

1 Cf. my *Ethics: Inventing Right and Wrong* (Penguin, 1977), chapter 1.
2 See J. O. Urmson, *The Emotive Theory of Ethics* (Hutchinson, London, 1968) and R. M. Hare, *The Language of Morals* (Oxford, 1952).
3 J. Harrison, *Hume's Moral Epistemology* (Oxford, 1976), pp. 13–15.
4 Price, in particular, firmly held this view. He quotes with approval the statement of Dr. Adams, that 'to perceive an action to be right, is to see a reason for doing it in the action itself, abstracted from all other considerations whatsoever'. R. Price, *A Review of the Principal Questions in Morals*, edited by D. D. Raphael (Oxford, 1948), p. 117 note.
5 This reading is also supported by Hume's immediately following claim that 'this discovery in morals, like that other in physics, is to be regarded as a considerable advancement of the speculative sciences'. Merely to report what people already mean could hardly be such an advancement.
6 Theses, 3, 4, 5 and 6 must be read as denying that moral judgments have the tasks mentioned as their sole function. For example, 6 says that the meaning of a moral judgment is not exhausted by the expression of any set of beliefs; it does not deny that a moral judgment may combine the expression of a belief with that of a sentiment.
7 Cf. R. M. Hare, *op. cit.*, p. 29, and *Freedom and Reason* (Oxford, 1963), p. 2.
8 See G. R. Grice, 'Hume's Law', in *Aristotelian Society Supplementary Volume*, XLIV (1970); J. R. Searle, 'How to derive "ought" from "is" ', in *Philosophical Review*, 73 (1964), also *Speech Acts* (Cambridge, 1969); R. M. Hare, 'The Promising Game', in *Theories of Ethics*, edited by P. Foot (Oxford, 1967), where Searle's article is also reprinted; and chapter 3 of my *Ethics: Inventing Right and Wrong* (Penguin, 1977).

V VARIANTS OF SENTIMENTALISM (*TREATISE* III i 2)

1 J. Harrison, *Hume's Moral Epistemology* (Oxford, 1976), p. 114.
2 R. M. Hare, *Freedom and Reason* (Oxford, 1963), especially chapters 2 and 3; Hare's view is what I call below a mixed account.
3 Cf. my *Ethics: Inventing Right and Wrong* (Penguin, 1977), pp. 30–5.
4 Cf. E. Westermarck, *Ethical Relativity* (London, 1932), and chapter 1 of my *Ethics: Inventing Right and Wrong*.
5 The question of what analysis of evaluations is implicit in the *Treatise* is discussed by Harrison, *op. cit.*, chapter VII, by Páll S. Árdal in chapter 9 of *Passion and Value in Hume's Treatise* (Edinburgh, 1966), and by Philip Mercer in chapter III of *Sympathy and Ethics* (Oxford, 1972).
6 The possibilities of quasi-realism are fully argued (with some reference to Hume) by Simon Blackburn in 'Truth, Realism, and the Regulation of Theory', in *Midwest Studies in Philosophy*, V (1980).

VI THE ARTIFICIAL VIRTUES (*TREATISE* III ii 1–12)

1 See E. F. Carritt, *Ethical and Political Thinking* (Oxford, 1947) pp. 37, 102–3; for Searle, see note 8 to chapter IV above. Cf. A. N. Prior, *Logic and the Basis of Ethics* (Oxford, 1949), chapter 5.
2 I have discussed Searle's argument in my *Ethics: Inventing Right and Wrong* (Penguin, 1977), pp. 66–73. When I speak of someone who 'endorses the institution', I do not mean one who merely approves of it or thinks that it is beneficial, but rather one who thinks and speaks from within the institution. Suppose that there is some established practice in terms of which A can place B under an obligation by saying so in appropriate circumstances; then anyone who adopts the ways of thinking and speaking that help to constitute this practice will indeed say that when A has done this B is under that obligation. But this variant brings out, more obviously than the practice of promising itself, that it is not the mere verbal trick of an explicit performative which creates the obligation, nor even the existence, as a sociological fact, of the relevant practice. Someone who recognizes both of these still has the choice either to stand outside the institution or to step inside it, and only if he makes this further optional move of stepping inside the institution will he seriously assert that B is under this obligation.
3 *Leviathan*, chapter 20, paragraph 2.
4 *Ethics: Inventing Right and Wrong*, pp. 184–5.

VII THE NATURAL VIRTUES (*TREATISE* III iii 1–5)

1 *Enquiry*, section V, part ii, note. There might seem to be a conflict between Hume's claim in *Treatise* II i 11 that ' 'Tis evident, that the idea, or rather impression of ourselves is always intimately present with us, and that our consciousness gives us so lively a conception of our own person, that 'tis not possible to imagine, that any thing can in this particular go beyond it' and

what he has said in *Treatise* I iv 6: '... nor have we any idea of *self*, after the manner it is here explained ... self or person is not any one impression, but that to which our several impressions and ideas are suppos'd to have a reference. ... It cannot, therefore, be from any of these impressions, or from any other, that the idea of self is deriv'd; and consequently there is no such idea.' This apparent conflict is resolved, however, by the fact that these two passages deal with two different notions of self. That of which it is denied in I iv 6 that we have any impression or idea is '*self*, after the manner it is here explained', that is something with 'perfect identity and simplicity' of which 'we are every moment intimately conscious', and such that 'we feel its existence and its continuance in existence'; Hume is denying that there is any awareness of a Cartesian *ego* that would immediately solve the problem of personal identity. But the self of which we are said in II i 11 to have a particularly lively impression is just the 'bundle of perceptions': 'This object is self, or the succession of related ideas and impressions, of which we have an intimate memory and consciousness' (II i 2). Similarly in II i 9 he says, '... pride and humility have the qualities of our mind and body, that is *self*, for their natural and more immediate causes.' So it is a Humean self the impression of which – that is, the series of impressions and ideas constituting which – is used to explain sympathy, pride, etc. throughout Books II and III, not the Cartesian self which was denied in Book I.

2 I. Kant, *Groundwork of the Metaphysic of Morals*, chapter 1. Jewels do sometimes shine by their own light. Robert Boyle discovered that some diamonds display photoluminescence, and Kant may well have known this.

3 J. S. Mill, *Utilitarianism*, chapter 2.

VIII   SOME SUCCESSORS: SMITH, PRICE, REID

1 Robert Burns, 'To a Louse':

> O wad some Pow'r the giftie gie us
> To see oursels as ithers see us!
> It wad frae mony a blunder free us,
> An' foolish notion!

2 That this is what Price intends is made clear by the explanation he gives later of various moral terms. '*Right, fit, ought, should, duty, obligation*, convey, then, ideas necessarily including one another' (708). '... *rectitude* is a *law* as well as a *rule* to us ... it not only *directs*, but *binds* all, as far as it is perceived' (713). See also Price's quotation from Dr. Adams, given in note 4 to chapter IV above, which, after saying that to perceive an action to be right is to see a reason for doing it in the action itself, apart from all extrinsic considerations, continues 'this acknowledged rectitude in the action, is the very essence of obligation, that which commands the approbation and choice, and binds the conscience of every rational being.' See Price's *Review*, p. 117.

3 G. E. Moore, *Principia Ethica* (Cambridge, 1903), chapter 1.

4 *Review*, pp. 81–3.

5 *Review*, p. 159.

6 R. M. Hare argues that they can be so reconciled and justified, e.g. in 'Principles', in *Aristotelian Society Proceedings*, LXXIII (1972–3) and 'What is wrong with slavery?', in *Philosophy and Public Affairs*, 8 (1979).

7 G. J. Warnock, *The Object of Morality* (Methuen, London, 1971), chapter 7.

8 This passage echoes what Hume himself says in Appendix 1 to the *Enquiry* (p. 290 in the Selby-Bigge edition).

IX CONCLUSIONS

1 I have here tried to allow for a view of moral concepts for which John McDowell has argued. But he sees it as an objection both to subjectivism or sentimentalism and to intuitionism of the kind I am here trying to clarify.

2 R. Dawkins, in *The Selfish Gene* (Oxford, 1976), uses 'meme' as a name analogous to 'gene' for the replicators that are selected in cultural evolution.

3 Dawkins (*op. cit.*) argues that socially beneficial genetic traits will not be selected as such, but I have argued that such 'group selection' is possible in certain favourable circumstances, and the same may hold for cultural traits. See my 'The Law of the Jungle: Moral Alternatives and Principles of Evolution', in *Philosophy*, 53 (1978).

4 Views like those in the *Enquiry* are expressed in the essays 'Of Passive Obedience' ('the obligation to justice is founded entirely on the interests of society') and 'Of the Original Contract'. ('The general interests or necessities of society are sufficient to establish both' – that is, both the obligation to allegiance and the obligation to keep promises – and 'If the reason be asked of the obedience which we are bound to pay to government, I readily answer, *because society could not otherwise subsist.*')

5 J. Bentham, *A Fragment on Government*, chapter 4, paragraphs 19–20 and 39–41.

6 As Thrasymachus says in Book I of Plato's *Republic.*

7 This case against morality is due mainly to Ian Hinckfuss, who, however, would state it far more vehemently.

INDEX

absolute power, 108
actions: can have representative function, 55; virtuous only as signs of motives, 79–80, 132
Adams, W., 158, 160
advantage of the stronger, 95, 155
allegiance, 106–13
Ardal, P., vii, 159
Aristotle, 16, 43, 128–9
artificial virtues, vii, 5, 28–9, 32, 63, 76–119, 145, 148
Austin, J. L., 20, 158
authoritative prescriptions, 22
authority of conscience, 37, 46

Balguy, J., 34–5
basic practice and moral overlay, 87, 100–1, 116–17, 149, 154
belief alone as motive to action, 53, 141–2
benevolence, 13, 25, 121, 126; three kinds, 28–9, 31, 35, 41–2; not contrary to self-love, 40; not the whole of virtue, 42, 137
Bentham, J., vii, 152–4, 161
Berkeley, G., 157–8
besieged city, 84, 93–4
Blackburn, S., 75, 159
Brown, K. C., 157
Burns, R., 131, 160
Butler, J., 13, 31, 35–43, 48, 54–5

Caesar, 128
calm passions, 47–8
Capet, Hugh, 112
Carritt, E. F., 98, 159

categorical imperatives, 12, 39, 133, 147; incorporated in linguistic rules, 62
chastity, 118–19
Christian morality, 117, 127
circumstances in which justice is or is not needed, 83–4
Clarke, S., 12–20, 34, 36, 47, 52–6, 82
communist utopia, 84
conceptual analysis, 6, 66–7
conflict resolution, 155
conscience, 36–7, 42–3, 46
contract theory of political obligation, 109–10
convention, 83, 88–90, 96, 99–103, 114, 117, 125, 132, 148–9
Cooper, Anthony Ashley, see Shaftesbury
co-ordination problems, 86, 88
Cromwell, Oliver, 112
Cudworth, R., 16–17

Dawkins, R., 157, 161
debauchees, 78, 92
democracy, 111, 113
demonstration and probability, 44
demonstration of morality, 56–7, 63, 135, 139, 141
desires not dependent on expected pleasure and pain, 46
determinism, 12, 128
dispositional descriptivism, 69–74, 143
duress, validity of promises made under, 104

education, 86, 101

163

equality, 86, 93
error theory of moral judgments, 52; *see also* objectification
evolution, biological and social, 80–2, 148–9

fitness, relations of, 15, 39, 48, 52
Foot, P., 158
free rider, 90

general scheme of justice only is beneficial, 81, 91
God as the basis of morality, vii, 16–17, 158
golden age, 83–4
good-breeding and etiquette as minor artificial virtues, 126
good will shines like a jewel, 124
government, 106–13, 155
gradations in everything natural, 105–6
gratitude, 101–2
greatness of mind, 125
Grice, G. R., 158
Guicciardini, Francesco, 128

Hanover, House of, 112
Hare, R. M., 70, 158–9, 161
Harrison, J., viii, 47, 54–5, 67, 158–9
Hinckfuss, I., 161
Hobbes, T., 7, 18–20, 82–3, 107–8, 115, 150–1, 159
honesty, 77–96
horrid crimes, 28
Hume's Law, vii, 61–3
Hume's works: 'A Dialogue', 67; *An Enquiry concerning the Principles of Morals*, 1–2, 65–7, 86, 93, 95, 153, 157, 159–60; *A Treatise of Human Nature*, *passim*; 'Of Passive Obedience', 161; 'Of the Original Contract', 109, 161; 'Of the Standard of Taste', 65, 67, 74
human nature as the basis of morality, 36–9
Hutcheson, F., 4, 24–35, 42, 82, 132, 134–5, 139, 151
hypothetical imperatives, 8–9

imagination, 95–6, 111, 155
immediate gains preferred, 107
impartial spectator, 67, 130
impartial system of moral sentiments and judgments, 66, 121–4, 127, 129
incest, 57

index-linked natural features, 146–7, 149–50
inflexibility of rules as proof of artificiality, 106
international system, 115–17, 155
intuitions and intuitionism, 19, 39, 54, 63, 135, 139, 145–7
is and *ought*, vii, 61–3, 98
Islam, 119

Jacobites, 112
James II, 112
jewels that shine by their own light, 124, 160
judge as feeler, 144, 150
judgments, conjoined with but distinct from feelings, 142–3
justice, 76–96; as giving everyone his due, 77, 104–5; international, 113–18

Kant, I.: on moral worth of actions, 31; on good will, 124, 158, 160

laws of nations, 113, 117
limited virtue, effects of, 28
linguistic communication shows sameness of meaning between persons, 142
Livy, 128
Locke, J., 32, 56, 58, 82, 135

McDowell, J. H., 161
Mandeville, B., 13, 23–4, 82–3
Mercer, P., 159
merit distinguished from propriety, 131
metaphysical ideas, due to the understanding, 134
Mill, J. S., 126, 160
misers, 84, 92
modesty, 118–19
Moore, G. E., vii, 54, 61, 133–4, 160
moral language, indeterminate in meaning, 68
moral phenomenology, viii, 43, 137, 139, 142
moral sense, 2, 3, 13–15, 25, 131–3; meaning of 'moral sense', 26, 32–3, 65–6
moral statements, meaning of, 65–75
morality, does more harm than good, 145, 154–6; is practical, not inert, 3, 52, 59, 68–9, 124; this queried, 54–5
motives only are virtuous, 79–80, 152

natural abilities, 127–8
natural selection, 80–1, 148–9
natural virtues, 3–5, 120–9; partly artificial,
  123–7; justice half natural, 85
naturalism, 54
Newton, I., 6, 157
non-cognitivism (non-descriptivism;
  emotivism and prescriptivism), 52,
  59–60, 69–71, 73, 143; in mixed theory,
  71
Noxon, J., 157

oak tree, 57
objectification, 71–5, 136, 143–4, 145,
  147–50
objectivism, vii, 13, 15–16, 33–5, 51,
  133–47, 150; smuggled in, 63
objectivity, claim to, 34–5, 74, 150; and
  quasi-realism, 75
obligation, placing oneself under, 98
open question argument, 134

pain, moral qualities compared with, 32–4
partial conflict, 88, 90, 150, 156
Passmore, J. A., 157
Plato, 161
Plutarch, 128
political obligation, 106–13
politicians invent or encourage virtues,
  23–4, 85–6, 101
Polybius, 128
postulated entities (calm passions, fitnesses),
  49
practice as the unit of choice, 92
Price, R., vii, 19, 43, 54, 99, 132–9, 160
Prichard, H. A., 54
pride, 125
primary qualities, moral qualities compared
  with, 32, 51, 61
princes, moral rules for, 113–15
Prior, A. N., viii, 159
prisoners' dilemma, 10, 86, 88–90
promises, 96–104, 155; promise breaking
  as contradiction, 98; promise keeping as
  veracity, 138; promising as an act of the
  mind, 98–9; as involving a fiction,
  103–4
property, 76–96; rules which determine,
  94–6; uniformity of rules, 93–4, 154
propriety distinguished from merit, 131
psychological explanation, 6, 120–3, 130–2
psychology of action, 1–2, 44–50

quasi-realism, 75

Raphael, D. D., viii, 157–8
rational principles of action, 140–1
rationalists, 15
rationality, selfish, 11, 78, 83–90, 99–100,
  114–17, 140, 150–1
reason, inert, 3, 52; the slave of the
  passions, 1, 45; conflict with passion,
  44–6, 49; not the basis of morality, 2,
  51–63; meaning of 'reason', 51, 140
redistributive taxation, 93
Reid, T., vii, 19, 54, 58, 139–44
representative function, distinguishes
  statements and reason from actions and
  passions, 55
retributivism, 137–8
rights, 28, 30, 137–8, 154–5
robbers, moral ideas of, 27
Rob Roy, 127
Roman law, 94–5
Ross, W. D., 54

Searle, J., 62, 98, 159
secondary qualities, moral qualities
  compared with, 51, 58, 64, 66, 136
seditious bigots, 84, 92, 155
seeing ourselves as others see us, 131, 160
Selby-Bigge, L. A., 158
self, idea or impression of, 121, 159–60
self-esteem a virtue, 125–6
self-love: defended by Butler, 41; rational
  superiority of, 37–8, 41, 46; restrains
  itself, 83
selfishness (total): asserted by Hobbes, 7; by
  Mandeville, 23–4; denied by
  Shaftesbury, 13–15; by Hutcheson,
  25–6; by Butler, 36–7, 39–40
sense of duty, 77–9
sentiment as judgment or as feeling, 143
'sentiment of the understanding, or a
  perception of the heart', 43, 48, 55, 137
sentimentalism, variants of, 64–75, 122
sentiments as motives to action, 68
Shaftesbury (Anthony Ashley Cooper, 3rd
  Earl), 13–15, 20; criticized by Berkeley,
  157–8
Smith, Adam, 67, 130–2
society, men are made for, 37
sociological explanation, 6, 123, 132
sovereign, 10, 12, 86, 88–9, 150–1
special moral sense, 26; argument against,
  131

state of nature, 8, 83–4
states as inadequate individuals with
    diminished responsibility, 116
subjectivism, 74–5, 132, 137
supervenience, 19, 146–7
sympathy, 5, 13, 85, 120–1, 124–5, 130–2,
    149

Thrasymachus, 161
two men in a boat, 88–90

understanding as a source of ideas, 134;
    discovers necessary truths of
    supervenience, 147
United Nations, 116
Urmson, J. O., 158

utilitarianism, vii, 29–30, 92, 117, 127,
    138; in Hume, 151–4; unpalatable
    consequences of, 30, 137
utility, 95–6, 151–4, 161

value-blind Martian, 146
virtues, natural and artificial distinguished,
    3, 81
voluntary and involuntary action, 128

war, 113–15; impossible without morality,
    154
Warnock, G. J., 138, 161
Westermarck, E., 159
William III, 112
willing an obligation, 97, 103
Wollaston, W., 20–3, 52, 55–6, 82–3, 139